THIS IS ME

I AM...

HOPES AND FEARS

Edited By Byron Tobolik

First published in Great Britain in 2024 by:

Young Writers
Remus House
Coltsfoot Drive
Peterborough
PE2 9BF
Telephone: 01733 890066
Website: www.youngwriters.co.uk

Book Design by Ashley Janson

Softback ISBN 978-1-83565-192-6

Printed and bound in the UK by BookPrintingUK
Website: www.bookprintinguk.com
YB0579F

AMBITIOUS
OPTIMISTIC
LONELY
CREATIVE
KIND
PROUD
ANGRY
SHY HAPPY
LOYAL ANXIOUS
PASSIONATE
CONFIDENT
STRONG
ADVENTUROUS
BRAVE BORED
FEARLESS
SENSITIVE
EXTROVERTED
INTROVERTED
SAD STRESSED
AFRAID
MISUNDERSTOOD
FRUSTRATED

FOREWORD

Since 1991, here at Young Writers we have celebrated the awesome power of creative writing, especially in young adults where it can serve as a vital method of expressing their emotions and views about the world around them. In every poem we see the effort and thought that each student published in this book has put into their work and by creating this anthology we hope to encourage them further with the ultimate goal of sparking a life-long love of writing.

Our latest competition for secondary school students, This Is Me: I Am..., challenged young writers to write about themselves, considering what makes them unique and expressing themselves freely and honestly, something which is so important for these young adults to feel confident and listened to. There were no restrictions on style or subject so you will find an anthology brimming with a variety of poetic styles and topics. We hope you find it as absorbing as we have.

We encourage young writers to express themselves and address subjects that matter to them, which sometimes means writing about sensitive or contentious topics. If you have been affected by any issues raised in this book, details on where to find help can be found at www.youngwriters.co.uk/info/other/contact-lines

CONTENTS

DIFFERENT RELAXED
STRONG FIERCE
OPTIMISTIC
PASSIONATE
ANXIOUS

FUN LONELY
POSITIVE
ADVENTUROUS
HAPPY

THE POEMS

EXTROVERTED
FEARLESS
LOYAL
MISUNDERSTOOD
GRATEFUL
STRONG
UPBEAT

OK
FINE
TOUGH
BORED
SAD
WISE
CHILL
BRAVE
KIND
WISE
QUIET

STRESSED
AMBITIOUS
ANGRY
PROUD
INTROVERTED
ENERGETIC
TRUSTWORTHY

Autism

Autism can be hard to get diagnosed
It's a chemical imbalance that some don't know
Sometimes it feels like you're all alone
This poem is to make it more known.
Hypersensitivity, where do I start?
Getting overstimulated makes you rather aggravated
Smells can be strong like tastes on your tongue
Noises get too much sometimes,
It's hard to describe the pain inside.
Textures are a funny one, whether it is touching or eating
It can be a crazy feeling that can send your heart beating.
Some of us can speak a lot and others may not
Eye contact is a strange one,
Some give it all and some do not at all.
Heads can be busy like you're in a city
When you need concentration, this is a pity.
Thinking over thoughts that don't really matter
Feels like your brain's always having a natter.
Busy places make you feel scared and small
Everyone around you is so big and tall.
You get the feeling you don't really want to be out
Telling yourself, "Please, don't shout!"
Listen, I promise all will be okay!
You are not alone, so let's make that known.

Maizie Roscoe (11)
Albany Academy, Chorley

Me, Myself And I

I am losing hope
I am feeling so lost
I don't know how I am going to cope
I am struggling
At my lowest
Slowly giving up
But of course, no one noticed.
I am being attacked by my own thoughts
I am losing my battle
Sick and tired
Forgetting how to tread water
So I guess it's time to drown, either now or later.
But then...
I met you and you are amazing
The reason I got through
Saved me and my soul
Forever grateful
You are on my mind, night and day
And every time in-between.
You got me through everything that was painful
You were there for me
An angel
Made me feel worthy
Not sure how I'd live without you
You've helped me through every tough journey

My lifeline
Guided me home in the dark
I trust you with every little part of my heart
You were that spark
The spark which enlightened me
I just want to say, thank you.
The light in finding my truth
I am beyond happy to have you
I love you
Do you know who it is?
That person is...
Me, myself and I.

Fatimah Akram (11)
Albany Academy, Chorley

The End

A love gone so soon,
What I once had faith in and worshipped,
Had passed in time,
A bitter change,
That transformed me.

Through so much pain and suffering,
I had gone,
So much loss,
And death to relationships passed by,
A war of emotions fizzled.

Hate, sadness, anger, bitterness,
Once all negative emotions lived within me,
But every now and then,
I'd escape to the wilderness,
Get away from all thoughts and fears,
There, is where I felt safe,
There, is where I could bare my face,
There, was my sense of place.

Sam Fitzharris (15)
Albany Academy, Chorley

This Is Me

My name is Amelia
And I am eleven

Dancing since I was seven
Freestyle
Commercial too

Dancing makes me happy
But my favourite thing to do is
Party!

I love holidays
Set your mind free
To do your favourite things
Completely stress-free

Pink, purple, blue
I love a barbeque
Particularly with my whole family
And maybe even you?

This was a poem all about me.
How about you?

Amelia McGeehan (11)
Albany Academy, Chorley

Me

I am a complex human being,
With limited interests - I am told,
I like Lego, Star Wars and reading,
After my diagnosis at 10 years old.

My attention to detail is great,
Not a fan of loud sounds,
I struggle if I am late,
I prefer fewer people to be around.

Change can be hard,
Because routine is important to me,
My superpowers become marred,
That's right, I'm Theo G!

Theo Grady (11)
Albany Academy, Chorley

I Am Nice

I am nice,
But not when I'm angry,
I am a sweet type of person,
I don't really like tangy,
I am a goalkeeper,
Diving left and right,
Sometimes I can't save some of them,
Because the goals are always tight,
I am a gamer,
Playing FIFA makes me happy,
But when they score and Griddy,
I always say, "That's jammy."

Ethan Lancaster (11)
Albany Academy, Chorley

I Am Me

I am weird,
I am kooky,
(Some people even call me spooky).
I am strong,
I am brave,
I am nobody's slave.
I am proud,
I am loud,
(Although my head is always in the clouds).

And I know I am different,
I don't care,
I am me,
I am perfect just as I am.

Lucy Forshaw (11)
Albany Academy, Chorley

The Hands Of Our Clock

One by one,
The day is done,
Tick, tick, tick,
Go the hands of the clock,

Hour by hour,
Day by day,
We watch our memories,
Slowly float away,

But these memories say,
Don't let us wash away,
Watch me flourish,
Watch me grow,
Until our time eventually goes,

Time will come,
Time will fade,
Don't let these memories,
Be of the past again,

This is our day.

Eva Roberts (12)
Aldercar High School, Langley Mill

This Is Me

This is me
Me is this

A kind, bubbly girl
Who used to be a
Sweet, shy nobody
A star waiting to shine
A spy undercover

But look at me now
A smart, sassy girl
The rainbow in the rain
The pink flower in a field of daffodils

Yes, you heard me right
I'm unique
Some might say
I'm one of a kind

I laugh in the rain
Cry at adverts
I make jokes with my friends that no one else understands
But that doesn't make me weird or different
It makes me, me!

Imogen Griffiths (11)
Alun School, Mold

Netball

Passing with class
Spring on the attack
Bring on the defence.
Score, pivot, rebound and jump!
Be a good sport on the court
No cautions or warnings.

Defend and attack till the end.
Intercept and drive
Find space,
No diagonal passes
Ball above your head on the centre pass.

Look for GA and WA
If marked, look for GD, WD
Well... that's what I do.

Defend, shoot and celebrate.
Your team has won
At its best.

Mali Wyn Davies (11)
Alun School, Mold

The World's A Book

Pages turned,
Bridges burned,
The world's a book from which I learn.

I craft my life,
A sharpened knife,
Its blade cutting through all my strife.

People will push me down,
People will make me frown,
But one day, I'll be too big to hit,
Too good to shoot, towering over you.

So why don't you just let me be?
Let me be free,
Without paying your fee,
Let me be me.

Sofia Jelley (12)
Alun School, Mold

An Idea

An idea so delightful,
The result ever so frightful,
A list of enemies,
Not remedies.

A recluse, hiding away,
Someone missing day by day,
Artwork of things unjust
Of something in a river, collecting rust.

Sophia Jones (13)
Alun School, Mold

Me

This is me.
I'm so small.
This is the world.
It's so big.
This is life.
There is no clear path ahead.
Making it up as I go
Not knowing where I'm being led.
And in-between all of that
I'm still me,
And this is still my life
And I wouldn't ask for anything better.
I love me.
I love my life.

Mia Shore
Ansford Academy, Castle Cary

This Is Me

I am optimistic with a dollop of passionate.
I am creative with a hint of shy.
I am loyal with a sprinkle of kind.
I am extroverted with a dash of introvert.
I am confident with a pinch of adventurous.
I am me, Elisha.

Elisha Hughes (12)
Ansford Academy, Castle Cary

Us?

"There's no such thing as normal,"
That's what I tell myself every morning in the bathroom mirror.
When you're my age, it's tricky to find who you are.
It's like looking through a deck of cards trying to find the right one to place down.
It's like sailing a ship through an ocean trying to find an island.
Emotions are a key part of who we are.
Faces and actions are good for hiding them.
How we look is different from how we feel.
Our minds always rely on stereotypes.
We think that there are only a few types of people in this world, yet there are many.
I don't know who I am yet, but I will find out,
And so will all of you reading this poem.
I leave saying this and I'm not going to say, be yourself.
That advice is too old-fashioned.
Because do we really know who we are yet?

Evie Sansom (14)
Aurora Eccles School, Eccles

About Me

My name is Grace and I like eating grapes.
I like watching Bluey and playing with something gooey.
My hair is blonde and I have a bronze medal.
I have green eyes, I was on the scene.
I dislike tomatoes and mash made from potatoes.
My favourite colour is blue and I like to chew gum.
I like to run, then eat a sweet bun.
I saw a rainbow out of the window.
I had a hot dog last week and I have a dog in my house.
I have a sister with a blister.
I have a brother who wants to stay with his mother.
My favourite animal is an octopus.
My nana and grandad like to travel on a bus.

Grace Helwin (13)
Aurora Eccles School, Eccles

This Is Me

Cats and dogs are both equally liked,
Summer is the season that everyone likes,
Hermoine Granger is the best,
Quiz me on Harry Potter and Star Wars,
I'm sure I'm up to the test,
Musicals are my style,
I would wear dresses and skirts all the while,
Chocolate and sweets are super tasty,
So is chocolate pastry.

Summer-Dawn Smart (13)
Aurora Eccles School, Eccles

Theatre

T he
H ouse of
E normous
A ctors
T ouring
R ound
E arth.

Logan Nuttall (13)
Aurora Eccles School, Eccles

The Truth Untold - The Real Me

In the crevices of my heart, a secret did reside,
A truth untold, waiting patiently inside.
For too long I've hidden, afraid to let it show,
But now I'm ready, it's time for the world to know.

With sweaty palms and a soul to set free,
I step into the light, revealing *the real me.*
Through my doubts and fears, I've managed to find my way
To embrace the truth, with courage on display.

To my family, near and dear,
I share this truth, so sincere.
For in your hearts, I hope you'll see,
The person I've always been, *the real me.*

So here I am, standing tall and true,
Sharing my story to all of you.
With this newfound freedom, I can confidently say,
I am proud of who I am every single day.

Darcey Woodhatch (15)
Belmont School, Holmbury St Mary

A Peculiar Premise

Chatter in the inconstant air
Comes to me like an unrequited surprise
Like jealous eyes to a jewel
That costs twice but no fare
Illuminating the clouds of blunt knives

Pure but no less than fuel
Like pixelated pixies pursuing a dare
Envious animals, yet impossible to derive
From their dark shrouded lives

Hush - the sound reappears like a euphoric nightmare
Wavering my attention like a lover from a duel
Diverting me from destiny's fool;

The song stops. Halted as quickly as it cultivated,
Stuck somewhere deep within the depths of the screen.

Oskar Larsen-Jackson (15)
Belmont School, Holmbury St Mary

Love's Embrace

In the realms of life where hearts entwine,
A tale of love begins to shine.
Where souls unite in gentle dance,
Embracing fate's enchanting chance.

Love an ethereal cosmic force,
Guiding us on our destined course.
It knows no bounds, no time nor space,
A transcendent bond we can't erase.

With tender touch and whispered sighs,
Love paints the world with vibrant dyes.
It blooms like flowers, kissed by dew,
Bringing joy and healing through.

Love is a symphony of trust,
In its embrace, we become robust.
The power to heal and to forgive,
To help each other truly live.

It's not confined to just romance,
But found in friendship's sweet expanse.
Love bridges gaps and mends divides,
A beacon of hope that always abides.

Yet love can also cause us pain,
Leaving scars that still remain.
But within the darkness, it reveals,
Strength and growth, like tempered steel.

So let us cherish love's embrace,
For in its light, we find our grace.
May it inspire and set us free,
To love ourselves and others endlessly.

For love's the essence of our being,
A gift worth seeing, worth decreeing.
In every heart, it yearns to reside,
A flame eternal, forever beside.

Kai Foster (16)
Bexhill Academy, Bexhill-On-Sea

The Real Me

The real me,
Is being haunted
By all these thoughts trapped inside.
Will there be a change?
I constantly ask
Those memories
Do they define me?
Flashbacks, reminding me of the things
I wish to forget.
However, they're on constant replay,
My mind forcing me to rewatch
Over and over and over again.
The real me,
Isn't who you see at school.
The real me,
Isn't who you see on the streets.
The real me,
Isn't even seen at home.
You see what I want you to see.
I end up getting lost in these personalities,
I have created for you.
I wonder,
Do I know who I am?
Do I even know,
The real me?

Luna Ribeiro (14)
Bishopshalt School, Hillingdon

This Is Me!

I'm Millie Kneale and here's the deal.

I was born on the Isle of Man
And I'm a massive 80's music fan.
My parents always say I was born in the wrong year -
My obsession with the 80s is severe.
I love listening to Nirvana
And I have a real passion for drama.

I struggle a lot with my mental health,
But I'm learning to focus on myself.
I've been to my fair share of therapy
And now I feel like I've improved mentally.
When I'm feeling blue,
I'll walk my dog by the sea with a view.

My favourite sport is netball,
And the best time of year is when the orange leaves fall.
Tim Burton films are my ideal movies -
I'd rather watch them than go out and spend my parents' money.

When I grow up, I want to be a therapist -
Or something similar to a children's specialist.
I want to help kids and adolescents who struggle,
So I can help them cope and keep them out of trouble.

Millie Kneale (14)
Castle Rushen High School, Isle Of Man

Decisions

Decisions are what make us
If people want to tear themselves
Or the world
Apart
Or strive for something greater than themselves,
Stained on themselves forever.
Decisions are cruel deceptions,
Bait from a taunting universe
Put in the hands of the horrendous nature
Of humankind,
Dangling the beautiful potential
Of that wonderful future of 'If'.
For me, decisions stay as something untouchable,
Something I have no say on,
Like a child shooed away from
A dinner's late-night talk
Because the adults are talking,
Unknowing or uncaring that she could still hear.
I find myself gazing
Into that wonderful world of
'If'.
I see it in the clear blue sky
That shines with unjudged possibility,
Free from the condemning eyes of
Them.

"How will that help you in the future?" they taunt
Dragging my wings down
And further away from 'If'.
"You'll just try it once"
The lie used so many times, I know it closely.
I go to tea with it,
I invite it back home to chat with.
I could say no,
Put my foot down,
But unlike Icarus, I fear the sun,
Fear the shadows I will cast on them,
Fear their judgement weighing my wax wings down
And I plummet from the heavenly 'If'.
No fallen angel,
For at least they knew how to fly.
In the car to another
'One-time' activity,
I feel my clipped wings ache.
I look to the sky
And dark clouds obscure my vision.

Gigi Fisk (14)
Castle Rushen High School, Isle Of Man

It's Funny How...

It's funny how people change.
It's funny how that one person's emotions can change and it's not you.
It's funny how that person's opinions now change when they are in another group.
It's funny how that person, who you thought you could trust, will now talk about you when you're not there.
It's funny how they will now hear something about you and are immediately convinced it's true.
It's funny how they stop hanging out with you, start ignoring you, and are now completely avoiding you.
It's funny how we've gone from being best friends to strangers in less than a week.
It's funny how we don't speak anymore.
It's funny how I don't like you anymore, not anything about you.
It's funny how I don't know you.
It's funny how we aren't friends, not even companions.
It's funny how it's almost like you are one of those girls that we used to talk about, but it's not almost, it is.
It's funny how much you have changed.
It's funny how I won't change. This is me.

Ortensia Littlewood (13)
Cheltenham College, Cheltenham

This Is Me

I really like to
Read, read, read!
It definitely keeps me busy.
I also really like
Maths, maths, maths!
(Don't ask why, I just do!)
Also, I find science very
Fun, fun, fun!
Especially when we do practicals.
But I'm not as bothered about history -
It really can get a bit boring.
French isn't that
Bad, bad, bad!
But sometimes it can get confusing.
School overall is
Good, good, good!
(And I'm glad we don't need to come on weekends!).

Zuzia Jones (11)
De Warenne Academy, Conisbrough

This Is Me

This will be all about me,
As you might see.
I am kind of confusing,
Which I think is rather amusing,
Since I like things without much meaning.
I also like reading,
Although books most people loathe,
There are some funny little stories,
Like Three Little Goats!
However, I dislike bikes,
And also trikes -
I'm scared I might trip,
Maybe even slip,
And then my bike would be a tip!
This was all about me,
As you can now see.

Katie Bradley (11)
De Warenne Academy, Conisbrough

Just Imagine

Just imagine my life for a moment,
Where it feels as if time has stood still,
As I wonder about stuff that never even mattered,
And yet, as many thoughts turn my brain into a well,
Forever built to hold my complaints and emotions,
I feel the feelings I have for you,
Creeping up on me,
Secretly waiting for you to appear,
To flood my brain with feelings, with memories,
And many emotions,
And as I try to think of how to describe these sensations that float like bubbles, I realise there are no words that could explain my passion for you,
To taste your lips, to feel your tongue,
To know what your eyes see when you look at me,
But my love for you,
It will never be reciprocated,
So I cry myself to sleep,
Knowing your silky voice will never be able to catch my tears before they fall,
And all I can do,
Is just imagine what our love would be like,
Just imagining.

Kieran Winstanley (13)
Derby Cathedral School, Derby

This Is Me

There's been times that I've been crying my eyes out
And someone comes in, I wipe my eyes
And say it's fine
I think to myself, *Why are you lying?*
This is tiring
Feeling alone in a room full of people
Sometimes I feel like I'm in a sequel
After the good, now it's the evil
Eating me slowly, I need a Stitch like Lilo
This was supposed to be a poem about me
But really, maintaining privacy is all that I need
So you see, I really can't get too deep
On the subject that defines me
The subject of me
I'm an odd mix of sometimes craving intimacy
But at the same time, I push away viscerally
I stay silent, then act out belligerently
And then people think I'm doing this deliberately
Additionally, to be fair, the only thing I like is literacy
My passion for this shines bright and unequivocally
I feel like it's getting dimmed
There are people in my space
That'll leave me in disgrace
These lying, two-faced, insecure snakes
I'm full to the brim

People leave at a whim
The situation's looking grim
So many losses, no wins
Problems of life, I drown 'cause I can't even swim
And it's pretty ironic that I'm popular
So many problems that I'm faced with on the regular
Tryna be better, watching motivationals and seminars
Your words are a noose holding me by the jugular
And I feel like I'm back to the place that I don't want to be
I'm tired of all these fakes and all these wannabes
Aren't you tired of playing pretend? If not you, then defo me
I know I need help, I don't need sympathy
This is me
Beneath the surface, storms overtaking me
Feel like I let down my fam
Put a fake picture on the 'Gram
And then you envy, "Oh wow, she's glam."
This is me
There are different sides to me
Tired of people lying to me
All of this is tiring
People say I'm inspiring
But I'm down like you too
Think I'm perfect? You're a fool
I hope I introduced
And gave you a prelude
This is me.

Hadassah Adefuye (13)
Derby Cathedral School, Derby

My Little Farewell

When I start adulthood without you,
Know that I'm here,
All in agony for you,
I know you yearn, saying I'm not gone,
But how am I supposed to know?
You yearn, I wouldn't cry the way I did today this very day,
While thinking of those words we didn't say,
I know how much you loved me and I loved you,
I still love you, even after death,
Each day, you thought of me and your disease,
You knew I would miss you,
So when the morrow starts without you,
Know that I'm here,
All in whimpers for you,
I will try and comprehend that
A majestic creature came and took you away from me,
Oh, I barely told you goodbye,
It said your mansion was ready in heaven
Far above what we can imagine,
But as you turned away,
A wave of sorrow overshadowed you,
Tears struck you,
You knew I would miss you,
I will always love you,
You had so much to do,

So much to do,
I remember all of our days together,
The sweet and angry ones,
I thought of all the love we once shared,
The many laughs we shared,
If I could turn the clocks,
I would say goodbye, I would say goodbye,
Maybe see your smile,
Your beautiful laughter, I always heard,
By the end of the day, that can't happen,
When I thought of all the stuff you missed,
Like me going to secondary school,
I thought of you with a young heart filled with absolute sorrow,
We promised each other not another day filled with watching TV and no cycling,
Well, after all, you promised me emptiness,
You have been so trusting, so understanding,
Though there were some misunderstandings,
Some really stupid ones,
So when you are in heaven far above
Then we can imagine rejoicing,
Don't think you will not see me for one day
When I am very old, we will meet again
In the spiritual kingdom of the one and true God, Jesus.

Laura Destiny (11)
Derby Cathedral School, Derby

'Men'tal Health

It's the way we're raised,
It feels our emotions are just there for people to invalidate,
And we're never praised,
But all our failures, all our weaknesses,
They're served to us on a silver plate.
And they wonder why we're filled with rage,
Us, half-dead,
Some more, taught to fight and go to war,
But they never taught us how to battle the greatest enemy.
Now, I see your faces out there thinking,
Well, who's that?
As a matter of fact, it would be me.
Now, I'm not here for this,
All those pseudo feminists
Might tell me to sit,
But I'm here to talk about
What you told me not to.
That thing you can't see because you don't believe in it,
Or is it that you do believe and you feign ignorance to this ghost?
'Cause when it needed you the most, you weren't there.
You made it feel invisible and it was anything but.
Sitting, wallowing in its despair.
You turned the ghost into a poltergeist,
Causing more trouble than before.

Especially when it's alone.
You're the reason that ghost became what it is.
What you don't understand is that ghost isn't dead,
It's all too alive and it lives inside my head.
No one ever taught me,
So I had to teach myself.
But how can you teach,
Having never been taught yourself?
So I left it to the world to show me what to do.
But it only teaches women,
And the topic is very taboo.
How to let her go?
How to heal myself?
What's the key to wealth?
And why does no one talk about men's mental health?

Leland
Derby Cathedral School, Derby

Who I Am

You may not like me,
And I do not know why,
I may say I am fine,
But it does not mean I do not cry

Sometimes I feel too different
Like I do not belong here,
I often tell myself I am too different
Like I was born in the wrong year

I am only 11 and I may be autistic,
But I know that my dreams are nothing like my peers
I know what my dream is, my dream is to be a K-pop artist
And I want to say it *loud and clear*

So why can't I?

Is it because all I will hear is:
"Oh, why would you like that?"
"You will never do it, why don't you be a teacher or
something normal?"
"Oh, you like K-pop? All the boys look like girls and they are
talentless!"

I know that I am autistic,
That I like and think different things
To everyone else, but that doesn't mean
I don't have feelings

And I don't want to be heard by everyone
I want to be treated like a person
And I want that one person:
A friend, a partner,
But I can't help feeling like

I'm too weird to have one
I wish for no one to feel like I have
And still do feel that people are treated differently

Because they are black, white, girl, boy, neither, autistic, short, tall
No one is the same and no one should
Be treated like nothing.

Raiya Goodwin (11)
Derby Cathedral School, Derby

Just A Kid

A question that I ask every day,
I have a nice family,
I have a nice group of friends,
They all support me through thick and thin,
But only I can answer, 'Who am I?'
I know I'm a human,
I know I'm a child,
I know I'm a Muslim,
I also know I'm a weirdo,
But I don't know 'who I'm supposed to be'.
I want to make a change,
I want to help the unfortunate,
I want to put a smile on their faces,
I want to put a smile on my parents' faces,
But I also don't know 'how to achieve it'.
After writing this, I still don't know,
But what I do know is that I still
Have a long way to go,
After all, I'm just a kid.

Syeda Hurmat-E-Zahra Kazmi (11)
Derby Cathedral School, Derby

My Mother

My mother was always by my side,
She cared for me,
Held me in her arms as I cried,
Even when no one else did.

My mother, so pretty
Yet sassy, but still perfect,
Always glowing, always smiling,
I miss that now, more than ever.

My mother, my best friend.
"What's the difference?" they ask.
"Nothing! Nothing at all," I reply.

I will always love her unconditionally.

My mother.

I will always love her,
Always and forever.

Somer Chapple
Derby Cathedral School, Derby

I Am Many Things, But Mainly, I Am Me!

I am many things, but mainly I am me!
I'm a writer, I'm an artist, and I am free.
I am cool, I am kind, I'm a bit sensitive but that's fine.
I'm musical, I'm tall, I am loving, but that's not all.
I like school, I like home, I like playing on my phone.
Now here's something important, all about me,
I am vegan, here's the reason: I love all animals, the trees and the bees,
And I don't think animals should be locked in cages and eaten, you see.
But enough about that and more about me!
I sing, I dance around, I play with the dirt on the ground!
I'm a proud supporter of the LGBTQ+ community (Pride),
And that's not something that I'm going to hide.
If someone is mean to you or trying to beat you down,
Just remember this sentence to turn it around;
It will make you feel a bit better, I guarantee:
I am many things, but mainly, I am me!

Lorelei Weston (11)
Framingham Earl High School, Framingham Earl

This Is Me

This is me, Noah Mather,
I like football, video games and my family -
I have six cousins and one sister,
I also have a mum, a dad, two grandmas and one grandad.
My favourite football teams are: Man City, Huddersfield Town and the England national team.
My birthday is the 25th of October.
I have moved house six times (soon to be seven).
I *love* Greggs and eating together,
And my favourite sports are football, tennis and running.
I was born in Huddersfield, West Yorkshire.
I like going around my village, Stoke Holy Cross,
And my local city, Norwich.

Noah Mather (12)
Framingham Earl High School, Framingham Earl

This Is Me

This is me, Harry Loydall,
Born on the 4th of April 2011,
That makes me 12.

Likes:
I like karting, cars, Fortnite, Forza and so on and so forth.
I also like skiing and my cat 'cause I diss dogs too much.
I have been to France a lot and we're coming to the end of, could I say, touring it.
I love pizza, salad, burgers and stuff like that.
I do Scouts, which is good, 'cause I like doing productive things.

Dislikes:
Errrrrm, not much, but *dogs!*

Some of my friends:
Axl
Oscar
Fin
Kit
Nathen.

Harry Loydall (12)
Framingham Earl High School, Framingham Earl

This Is Me

My name is Eva Treby.
I like Heartstopper.
I like music, especially Baby Queen.
My favourite fictional character is Nicholas Nelson,
And my favourite drink is apple juice.
I enjoy going to theme parks and I enjoy photography.
My favourite lessons are English, art and food tech.
I like vans and I like Kaneko bags.
My favourite actor is Kit Connor,
I hope to meet him one day.
I am kind.
I am loyal.
This is me.

Eva Treby
Framingham Earl High School, Framingham Earl

This Is Me

I like cats, dogs and other pets.
I love gymnastics and acrobatics.
I'm so friendly,
I like to eat mashed potato and vegetables.

I'm from Ukraine, the city of Dnipro.
I have a cat and lots of friends,
And also a best friend,
Who has helped me everywhere,
It's Molly F.
I have grandparents and parents.
Now, I live in England.
I really like Poland and England.

Alisa Sliusarenko (12)
Framingham Earl High School, Framingham Earl

This Is Me, I Am...

T rouble when I'm with my best friend 24/7
H ave two fish and one dog
I 'm fun-loving and adventurous
S port is my happy place

I 'm kind and caring to everyone
S upporting my friends and family

M y dog called Bracken is my life
E xcited to try new things and go to new places.

Molly Forrest (13)
Framingham Earl High School, Framingham Earl

This Is Me

I love to draw,
I like to walk,
I like to read,
I love to talk.

Anon (13)
Framingham Earl High School, Framingham Earl

Smile

I smile with my crooked teeth,
As my mother does with hers.
She's still here, despite
The pain she held with her for years.
She had that strength,
She finally left.
And maybe we cry,
But together, we smile.

I smile with my crow's feet,
As my grandma does with hers.
She finds joy in all she does,
Her being radiates love.
Too much loss,
So her blue eyes cry.
But together, with our crow's feet,
We smile.

Granny Mum is my namesake,
Ramdassey Hajari Bancey.
We've never met,
But she has my utmost respect -
I know if she met the second Hajari,
She'd love me.
Together, Hajaris, we smile.
I smile with my sister's hand in mine,

She's small, but she's awesome and proud.
She knows what she wants,
Her work never stops.
We smile together,
And we smile loud.

Look at us standing tall,
Watch how we shine, even when we fall.
Acknowledge the tears that trail down our cheeks,
I'm opening my mouth so you can hear us speak.

One after the other,
All at once,
Together, we smile.

I Hajari Bancey (13)
Gladesmore Community School, Tottenham

The Culprit

One day while walking through Waterloo,
The weather was quite murky.
A Frenchman rolled right up to me,
And gave me a big fat leg of turkey.
The Frenchman was in a wheelchair,
With obvious disabilities.
But I knew I'd befriend him,
We'd have various possibilities.
He took a newt from his pocket,
I could see it was an amphibian.
It was a whopper to be sure,
It definitely wasn't size medium.

He stole the newt from the pond weed,
It was the size of an alligator.
He said he didn't steal it, but I could see,
He was the instigator.
I know this story makes no sense,
But I'll defend it from the pulpit.
If you find any bad grammar or spelling mistakes,
I'll defend myself from the pulpit!
My protesting will be in vain,
For obviously, I'm the culprit.

Joshua Keenan (11)
Gowerton School, Gowerton

All About Me

Hello, my name is Joseph,
I am 11,
And I like video games,
Even though they melt your brain.
I like rugby too,
But at the end of the match, I am tired and wet through.
I am loyal, proud and strong,
But sometimes I do stuff wrong.
I am happy too,
With all my friends, they help me pull through.
Though I underestimate my strength,
I try to keep it within the grabbing reach of my arm's length.
To keep it in check,
I also like the military: tanks, ships and planes galore,
But many of them can be old and worn.

This is me and I have many likes,
But most of all, I'm proud to be part-Welsh.

Joseph Feathers (11)
Gowerton School, Gowerton

The Rugby Match

A rugby match as tough as the Battle of Waterloo,
In the pouring rain, we knew what to do.
The coach shouted, "Pencil box and satchel!"
Moves we learned in secrecy,
To go against our formidable opponents.
Admittedly, the enemy in orange-coloured tops,
Were very slimy, like an alligator in the mud.
They had a dirty player, a culprit whose tackles
Were like severe torture,
But we got him with a whopper tackle.
He turned a greenish-grey colouring as he went down.
We won the game and shot to fame.

Ethan Davies (11)
Gowerton School, Gowerton

The Newt

I have a slimy newt
He is a torture to keep
He's a whopper of a newt
But he wriggled out of my hands
Someone cracked a garden pot,
He was the culprit of the job
Now he's my enemy and fairly, my friend.

Rhys Alexander (11)
Gowerton School, Gowerton

This Is Me

I have sometimes looked at myself
And said I can't do it
I thought I was fit for this
And I'm about to quit

But I hear a voice saying:
Don't give up, give it one more go
Although I'm not too sure,
I trust it and do so

I give it one more try
And it was right
Which just goes to show
To try new things, have no fright!

Christian Laudat (13)
Harris Academy, Beckenham

Resculpted

Because my imperfections are not pronounced as pretty by
the girls in my classes who are the definition of beauty,
The lump in my throat that was once sculpted by the gentle
hands of my peers
has now grown full out of space with guilt and indifference
that it's now tracing down my trachea, making its way into
my lungs as an easy route to my heart.
Taking over every winter with an overwhelming sense of
apathy and utter carelessness until it hits.
Realisation. How many people I love,
I've snapped at due to my selfish moments of self-
indulgence.
Just because I've had a bad day, doesn't make it their fault.
I wish to be resculpted, by the hands that smooth out the
lines in my face that have been so deeply carved by the
sharpest tool found by eye.
To fix the lines that seem so out of place and the petals of
clay-like skin overlapping each individual engraving.
To fix the way I look. Resculpted. I wish to be resculpted.

Sky (Marshall) Cornish (16)
Harris Girls' Academy Bromley, Beckenham

Morality

To be a member of the human race,
Swollen with the enigmatic complexities of human nature.
Naturally punctilious, I must bear the weight of mankind's original flame.
I possess the inquiring minds of those before me
Carrying the unfulfilled pursuit of the labyrinth of knowing and not knowing,
Where even the boundaries of curiosity and knowledge blur into obscurity, Where I'd fathom the essence of existing,
And unveil whichever unhidden truths that reside in us all.

Taylor Cooper
Harris Girls' Academy Bromley, Beckenham

She In The Waiting Office

Just one call
The call of her,
He has already gone,
You don't want that to happen to her too.

You worry,
You fear,
You fear the unknown,
Not knowing what will happen next.
Not again.

"It's okay," she says,
You know she is lying,
You think of all the things that can happen.
Over and over, wondering about the unknown.
She leaves you alone.
Not again.

Over and over, wondering about the unknown.
What will happen,
Not for her, she's been the best,
She is only young,
Not even 11,
Not 10,
Just turning 9.
Not again.

Too many beds,
One for every time she could never come back,
How could this happen?
How can this happen?

Ring, ring
Over and over,
Please answer.
Not again.

No operation,
No nothing.
No choice.
Not again.

Aminat Adekanmi (11)

Harris Girls' Academy Bromley, Beckenham

What People See

People look at me and see,
A confident girl without a care in the world,
A girl who doesn't need anyone...

People look at me and see,
Someone who is happy,
Someone who has no need to worry...

What people don't see is,
A small girl who worries 24/7,
Someone who always needs someone by her side.

What people don't see is,
Someone who is sad deep inside,
Someone who overthinks and worries about everything.

Sara Boutob (11)
Harris Girls' Academy Bromley, Beckenham

I Am Me

I can't stay quiet in this world of excitement,
The people, the books, such enlightenment.
But there is a point I need to make,
And this thing inside me cannot be caved.
I make a point and share my passion,
But deep down inside me, there are major distractions.
The cats and the geese are not my type,
So when I can, I follow the hype.
When writing stories for me, I felt,
Like a gorgeous Lindt chocolate beginning to melt.
So there you have it, my feelings and dreams,
And if we stay this way, we'll make a great team.
But when the time comes, we have to change,
Make the universe better, explore the range.
Those were the bricks that built me,
The memories that made me.
I am... *Me.*

Ava Henderson (12)
Heathside School, Weybridge

Who Am I?

Hello, I am Effie Glampedakis.

I lived in Greece,
And the blue skies I do miss
My favourite subjects: maths and science
Though I do like a bit of English.

Weybridge is my current home,
It's one of the best towns I've ever known
My dear family of six (including myself)
I have three younger sisters, all as sneaky as an elf!
I'm really scared of buzzing bees
But love what they do to help the plants and trees.

Swimming and basketball are my favourite sports.
Being an aeronautical engineer is my dream and hope!

Goodbye, I am Effie Glampedakis.

Effie Glampedakis (11)
Heathside School, Weybridge

My Family

We start off with me,
I like nature, including a bee.
Also, I like gymnastics,
When I land, it looks very neat,
It's like dancing to the beat.

We then go on a journey once more,
My sister likes the shore,
She also likes reading and finding out more.

We then go through nature once more,
To my mum; she likes tea,
She also loves me.

Lastly, we move on to our final branch of the family,
And it's my dad,
He plays golf and he's not too bad.

Isla Sceats (11)
Heathside School, Weybridge

Ice

As I glide across the ice,
It's like rolling some dice.
What would happen next?
I hope that it's my best.
A spin in the air,
They stand there and stare.
Would I land it, would I not?
Let's just see - fingers crossed.
Going skating in the crowded rink,
Our noses and cheeks go rosy pink.
What happens next - tumble and fall?
Don't I seem to understand it all?
What a wonderful winter treat,
One that's very hard to beat.
Finally, it had been a year,
Time to enjoy the winter cheer.

Taashvi Sood
Heathside School, Weybridge

Adventurous

A person who enjoys adventures,
D ragged in the mouth of a forest,
V olcanoes explored; voids jumped over,
E xcited every time,
N ot scared or frightened,
T ouching every rock,
U nder caves; over mountains,
R an through woods,
O n top of mountains,
U nusual animals spotted,
S pending almost every day exploring.

Heidi Lee (11)
Heathside School, Weybridge

Masterpiece

A drop of ink on the page
What colour next, maybe sage?
Will this become a masterpiece?
I guess we'll have to wait and see

A blob of ink on the brush
This time, let's try not to rush
As it strokes across the blank
The ink tries to spread its ominous black

A brush here, a brush there
Going on for hours on end
Finally, it's up on my wall
I think it's time to make the final call.

Yasmine Walshe (11)
Heathside School, Weybridge

This Is Me

I am brave,
I am strong,
I can do anything I put my mind to.

When my emotions take me away,
To a land far away,
I remember there are facts.

I am brave,
I am strong,
I can do anything I set my mind to.

My brown eyes, brown hair, my twin,
These are the bricks that create me,
And I never forget...

I am brave,
I am strong,
I can do anything I set my mind to.

Sophia Coville (11)
Heathside School, Weybridge

Languages

German and Mandarin
English, of course
Three languages I speak
With more coming soon
French and Spanish in a year or two
Oh, five languages, you say
But eight years it took
And a big bit of effort too
So now I say
Goodbye
Tschüss
Au revoir
Adios
Zaijian.

Jonathan Hartig (12)
Heathside School, Weybridge

What Will I Be?

What will I be?
How can I choose?
One option is an author,
With my mind in full control.
It's possible to be a gamer,
Lowering the lows and heightening the highs.
Letting myself be an artist,
In my very own world.
But to be honest,
Every option is open to me.

Laurie Milligan
Heathside School, Weybridge

This Is Me

H ong Kong
A Ravenclaw
Y es to *literacy!*
L oves to draw
E ntering the poetry competition
Y asss, Queen!

Hayley Chan
Heathside School, Weybridge

This Is Me

Dancing,
Dance, I do,
Delightfully drifting across the floor,
I love dancing,
And so do you.

Ellie Douglas (12)
Heathside School, Weybridge

The Ocean

A haiku

The ocean's shiny,
Such a wide range of creatures,
And coral reefs too.

Luke Gissendanner (11)
Heathside School, Weybridge

Cristiano Ronaldo

My idol is Cristiano Ronaldo and someday I hope to be like him because...

C oolest striker in the world
R eally good and does a lot for charity
I dol - he is my idol
S trong, fit, capable
T alented - a role model
I conic - the greatest footballer of a generation
A ged 38
N ever has given up
O nly tries his very best

R onaldo is a great example to me
O ffers his support to young people
N ike sponsors him because he is great
A lways, I will try to be like him
L egend!
D ynamite!
O h, Ronaldo - let's go.

This is who I want to be.

Connor Mitchell
Hillside School, Aberdour

Trailmakers

T railmakers is a great game which helps you learn
R eally good to gain experience in building
A nd it's creative
I know lots of people like it
L earn, experience and fun: the three things people will like about the game
M any opportunities to learn and create
A game that helps me grow and develop
K ids and parents will love it
E xcellent graphics, excellent design, excellent experience
R est, school, game, repeat - that's what I experience
S uper and a part of what makes me, me.

Robert Carr
Hillside School, Aberdour

My Life

I move about a lot,
It is difficult, so I have thought.
My mum means a lot to me,
We've grown together like a tree.
I want to be a pilot when I am old,
I would be good at it - I've been told.
Marvel, Lego, Pokémon and swimming,
Are all things I like - along with Stranger Things.
It is hard for me to be in care,
It can feel very unfair.
Some people help me,
To see.
That things can get better,
No matter the weather.
So today, I stand up tall,
And will always get up when I fall.

This is me!

Ryan Murray (11)
Hillside School, Aberdour

This Is Me

J am on toast is my favourite
A pples are nice
M y granny's dog is cute
I like fidget toys
E lephants, I like, because they're big and strong

J umping on trampolines is fun
U nder my blanket is where I am cosy
N ight-time is a fun time
I love Pokémon, especially Jiggly Puff
O nions make me cry
R unning around makes me tired.

Jamie Junior
Hillside School, Aberdour

This Is Me

L earning hard and finishing work,
E ach class is a challenge,
O nly need to focus on myself,
N ever tell lies or else!

S arah is my best teacher,
U nder the care of very nice people,
N eed to finish my work,
T eachers are always nice,
E ver naughty - in the chill room for you,
R eady for your classes, do them now!

Leon Sunter
Hillside School, Aberdour

Migraine

M ight not be a psycho, but I might go crazy
I 'm missing these messages telling me how to breathe
G oing crazy, acting like a criminal; I need medicine to heal my feelings
R age, healing - inside my heart's trapped soul
A nimal raging, uncontrollably
I nstability overruling me
N eed air
E xhausting me.

Dylan Dryden (11)
Hillside School, Aberdour

This Is Me

L evitating on a trampoline is fun
E ggs for breakfast make me strong
Y elling makes people hear me
L abrador is my favourite type of dog
A nd I love all animals
N o one can tell me monkeys aren't the best
D on't try to stop me being cheeky - this is me!

Leyland Stewart (12)
Hillside School, Aberdour

This Is Me

L ogan is my name
O scar is my friend and brother
G -Man is my nickname
A nd I'm cool
N *ever give up!*

Logan Stewart (11)
Hillside School, Aberdour

Questioning

This is me
A young questioning girl
Unsure of her life
School guiding the way
Like the point of a knife
This is me
The knife has a handle
So thin and so long
Made of emotions
Some weak and some strong
This is me
Happiness and worry
Sadness and fear
The girl seeks clarity
That has never been here
This is me
Her life path is yet to become
The blade of the knife
So strong and so sharp
Leading the way
Like the beat of a drum
This is me.

Isobel Wright (12)
Hoe Valley School, Woking

Growing Up

No one told me high school would be so different from that in my imagination,
Now I'm sitting here slowly getting closer to my graduation.

I always thought growing up would be a great thing,
I thought I could do whatever I wanted,
I could draw, write, play or even sing,
But no, I have to meet everyone's expectations along the way,
Like a puppy following the rules without any say.

I always thought I would still be friends with those from primary school,
Oh god, how could I be such a fool?
At first, we called every day,
Then we all started to drift away.
It turned into once a month,
To never again.
Like the past eight years just disappeared,
I guess that's something I had always feared.

Then we entered high school,
Everyone did whatever to be cool.
No one told me we were bringing our judgy selves,
If they did, I would have taken better care of myself.
I guess we all changed too much, way too fast,
We all just moved on right away from our past.

Before, bedtime was at eight,
I always thought that was so late.
Now my eyes are glued open until something after two,
Younger me would never believe this is true.
I used to wake up at seven-thirty,
Any time before that was way too early.
Now I'm awake before six,
Holding a concealer trying all the new tips,
Anything to hide my flaws.
It's my choice, it's not like it's also made into another law.

Except I'm surrounded by social media,
No little me, it's not the same as Wikipedia.
It's filled with lies,
It's filled with people commenting on each other's size.
I expected it to be more entertaining,
But instead, it became mentally draining.
So now I just leave people on delivered,
'Cause it's not like my feelings were ever considered.

Your smile may not be as bright,
And there may be bags under your eyes.
But at least now you're strong.
Little girl, this world isn't where you belong.

Stay strong,
Until the end.
The reward is better than the journey.
Just know I'll always be your friend.

Armeen Afridi (14)
Hoe Valley School, Woking

Blind To Character; The Illiteracy Barrier

Those who eschew literary pursuits
Are oft bereft of much-needed clues
To apprehend others' cogitations and views
Requires a level of perspicacity that ensues
From erudition gleaned through myriads of muse
So clutch a tome, let your intellect diffuse

In simpler words, do you really think you can understand me?
My words, my hopes, my emotions, my dreams, all entombed in a fragile, fleshy cage
When you don't read, don't understand, when you can't read, can't comprehend
My quirks, my perks, my jerks, the things I can't explain, so you have to do something on your part
I hope you've taken the time to read, to delve into my being
For when sometimes you can't read me, I become a raging fire ready to blaze

Sometimes I prefer to be left alone, reading, sleeping, thinking, depending on my mood
I'm not so good at making conversation, so I'll wait for you to initiate
Don't think I'm being pompous, I just have different facial expressions than you

I can't help it, but one of my talents is that I'm good at writing and being messy too
And my head nearly bursts at the seams, filled with fictitious stories and dreams

Words on a page, words spiralling in my mind, a portal to the realm of captivating thoughts
Ideas and musings, so easy to find, if you know where to look
Inspiration is bountiful, a wealth to unearth, for instance, a gem like this that shines:
The celestial stage brimming with shades of light and dark,
Planets and stars twirling in their unique way,
A mesmerising theatrical piece, for us to perceive and behold, like every human's world in their own right.

Nuha Khan (12)
Hoe Valley School, Woking

Everything Yet Nothing

I am everything yet nothing,
A dream and yet a drag,
A lighthouse in the darkness,
A narcissistic humble brag,

A multitude of parallels,
A myriad of lies,
A speaker in a silent place,
A devil in disguise.

I am everything yet nothing,
The one who waits and listens,
The diamond in the rough,
The one who condemns and christens,

The impediment of everything,
The exposure of my sins,
The final sand that shifts in the glass,
The epiphany at last begins.

I am everything yet nothing,
I am a lowly state of grace,
I am but made from the Holy God,
I am the one scorned in disgrace,

Yet why must I act so self-critical,
And why must I scorn and shame?
For who am I to disrespect,
My character, soul and name?

And so at last, I am transposed
Not everything yet nothing,
But this has come to perplex me:
Perhaps I may be something.

Emma Smith-Gould (14)
Hoe Valley School, Woking

Incomplete

I wanted to be like the girls in books,
And I guess in a way,
I already was,
Because nothing had been going right.

I was Olive without a hypothesis,
Macy with a love for books,

January with writer's block,
And Catalina being more tired than she looks.

I was Lily without an Atlas,
Tate waiting to be loved by Miles,

I wasn't on my sister's honeymoon,
There was no paintballing in sight,

No workplace enemies to lovers,
No childhood friends split up by a fight.

I was in brutal reality.

No love story to be told,
No responsibility to be had,
I was already twenty-three years old,

So, I lived in the books,
Wondering when my time would come,
As my story kept writing itself,
Each poetic line, one by one.

Lavinia Alves (14)
Hoe Valley School, Woking

Perspective

Roses are red, violets are blue
But that is just how we're taught, me and you
In this world, there's good and evil
A hero, a villain
But what is right and wrong is for you to decide
The truth might be buried deep within lies
A snake behind a lion's mask
A thief in a police uniform
What you see might not be right
Just truth hidden away with lies
So listen closely, think it through
And you might see the world differently too.

Winkie Lai (12)
Hoe Valley School, Woking

Living

If a dog, a cat and a mouse can live peacefully,
Then why can't we?
We always talk about kindness,
But we cannot fulfil that treaty.

So it's time to fill that gap between foe and friend,
By the time this is done, they'll be friends till the end.
They will laugh, joke and have company,
They will blend.

Forever, this poem will last,
I will cherish the past.

Manuella Brobbey (11)
Hoe Valley School, Woking

Falcon

I watched you gliding everywhere,
Wishing not to be you,
But your keen expanded wing,
Feeling the wind on top of everyone,
Suddenly, you left,
The only thing left was my love for you.

Pak Him (Isaac) Liu (11)
Hoe Valley School, Woking

Hallucinations Of Love, But Really Of Hate

I wake up in a forest,
The water droplets that slide down the leaves,
Strike down on the Earth.
I feel the vibration scatter from the core
And every time it punches the ground,
A small piece of heat breaks from the mini sun,
That lies and cries beneath us.
The waves hit like a truck,
But seem happy being finally released from their prison
I see a sea...

Before I manage to move a muscle,
I am snapped back to reality.
A lot has happened in my life,
The trees are the sticks of life,
Barely holding onto my emotions,
When a small piece breaks off and hits my world.
A big piece of my happiness breaks off,
And eventually, all my leaves are going to break off.
Rejected by the girl I loved and scarred by a 'loyal' friend,
That sea was a sea of roughness,
I could never have this,
Could anybody?

Neil Permal (14)
International Community School London, Paddington

I Am From

I am from tiny rooms and faded buildings,
From snowdrops, showing spring beginning.
I am from orange cars
And corrupt tsars.
I am from books piled up on every shelf.
I'm from the bowl
With my collection of seashells.
I am from Ladoga,
Brown sand and a clear cold lake,
From dumb mistakes.

I am from mandarins
For New Year's Eve,
From Harry Potter movies
Every winter night.

I am from swimming lessons
Twice a week,
And from Vatrushkas after it.
I'm from my mother,
English, maths,
I'm from my father,
Many laughs.
I am from dashing home from school,
From semolina kasha in the morning.

I am from anticipating growing up and leaving,
From knowing there's no place you yet belong.
And I'm from the sorrow of believing
You won't return, not anymore.

Daria Teterina (15)
International Community School London, Paddington

The Keys

When someone asks me,
"How many languages do you know?"
I tell them
I know two main ones:
English and music.
Whenever I sit down
On my black chair
Just a few centimetres away
From the reach of the black and white keys,
My brain shuts down, my hands develop their own little brains.
I play whichever note I want, it depends on my mood.
The black ones create an exotic atmosphere,
Making it feel like everything's pointless.
The white ones make you feel joy and innocence.
However, life has its ups and downs,
Having just one of them makes no sense,
You can't play if you don't have both black and white.
I place my hands on the keys and there it goes:
I can't control them anymore.
They will play until every single brain dies out.

Hulya Jabrayilzade
International Community School London, Paddington

Happiness

Happiness isn't found,
It is made,
Your dreams, hopes and ambitions,
Your family, friends and closest people to you,
This is happiness,
This is joy,
This is you.
So make memories with the people you love,
And chase your goals as if you are running out of time,
Because all of us slowly are,
Even if we don't always realise.

Stella Bunders (15)
International Community School London, Paddington

My Place To Be

The forest,
Silence and peace,
Is where I find relief,
I smell plants and trees,
I hear birds and leaves,
This is my happy place to be,
Insects are working,
While I'm exploring,
Finding my place to breathe,
To live,
To laugh,
To love,
To be safe once again,
The forest is my place to be.

Saana Seppala (14)
International Community School London, Paddington

This Is Me

This is me.
Creative, brave
Kindness given
Trustworthy, resilient
Loyal and brilliant

This is me.
Independent, fun
I love my Xbox One
Compassionate, smart
I like to do martial arts

This is me.
Unique, fair
Providing care
Mindful, motivated
Never frustrated

This is me.
Outstanding, nice
Giving out advice
Playful, polite
Filled with light.

Rohan Lewis (12)
Islwyn High School, Oakdale

I Am Exactly Who You Think I Am

I am boring, broad, brief and bleak,
I am but a clique.
I am lost, lucky, loud and lambent,
I am sitting in an encampment.
I am exactly who you think I am.

Robyn Aron Hughes (14)
Islwyn High School, Oakdale

The Satisfaction Of Music

H olding the headphones
E ndlessly searching for music
L ooking at one particular song
P eaceful. Peaceful. Peaceful.

M eaningful lyrics scatter across my brain
E volving into a trail of thoughts.

B ecoming an endless cycle of satisfaction
E nding in floods of tears
F inding myself after all these years
O f all the songs I see
R eprise is the one for me
E ager to stop the pain.

I n desperation to distract myself
T rying to escape
S atisfied at last, as music takes its pace.

T oo late to change
O pen to the damage
O pen to the heartbreak.

L istening to the instrumental end
A t last, my suffering is coming to an end
T hinking deeply about how to plead
E nding of the song, as my life begins to fade.

Ruby Warneck (14)
Kingswood Academy, Bransholme

Hiking

With every hiking trip, comes a list
Of things you need to pack.
A map so you don't get lost,
Some water to keep you hydrated,
Maybe even some activities to keep you entertained along the way,
But most importantly, all those things need to be carried in a bag.
A big, heavy boulder you are forced to carry on your journey,
Containing everything you need for a successful trip.
Along your way up the mountain,
Your bag begins to get heavier with each step you take
You stumble every once in a while but
You still manage to keep striving,
Striving towards your goal, which lies
At the top of the peak.
Sometimes if people see you struggling,
They offer to carry your bag for a little while,
But tend to give you it back when they
Start to feel drained and exhausted.
You never find a person who carries your bag permanently,
Someone who takes that weight off your shoulders.
You start to weep and feel weak at the knees,
Though you have only been walking an hour,
This trip is to last you an eternity.

An eternity of nothingness,
A lonely path you walk alone,
In the hope of finding a greater meaning in life,
A purpose,
A reason to go on.
And with that constant hefty pressure,
It starts to become too much.
Too much for you to handle on your own.
All those meaningless things you carelessly tossed into your bag,
Not realising the drastic impact it would have
On you in the future.
You regret it,
You regret all of it,
But it's too late.
Now, you have to carry it with you until the end.
If only you could go back and change things,
Things would be different.
You would be different.
You start to shout and push past the other climbers,
The ones who seemed to be enjoying their journey,
The ones who didn't put so much in their bags.
You wanted to reach the top before them,
To prove your purpose,
Your purpose on this journey.
But with all that stress and emptiness,
And all those regretful things you still have,

In your bag,
It's only a matter of time before you
Trip
And
Fall
And
Collapse.

Holly Mackman-Dalby (15)
Kingswood Academy, Bransholme

The Man I Met In Monte Carlo

There was a man I met in Monte Carlo,
Who was quick and as sharp as the sun.
But the Monte Carlo man was like a phantom,
Disappearing once the champagne was opened
At many of his lavish parties.
When he came to London in the summer of 1922,
When I myself was in my lesser and more vulnerable years,
The Monte Carlo man was a typical new money,
And oh, how I loved him.
But how could I love a man I had never met?
A man whose name I didn't even know.
It was only when I was out,
With a French cigarette and a glass of champagne,
I heard his name, which was only a surname,
But how Austen would have wept.
Abernathy.
When it was finally my turn for love,
I could never bring myself to walk to the altar
Because I had not fallen in love with my rich husband...
I had fallen in love with the man I met in Monte Carlo.

Ellis Williams (15)
Kingswood Academy, Bransholme

I, Me, Myself

People may see me as weird,
People may see me as odd,
I view me as different, in a good way.
It's a strength, a different view of the world.
I view myself as different characters.
Aziraphale, The Doctor, Sherlock Holmes,
Each one unique in their own way.
One's an angel, a principality,
Another's a Time Lord, travelling through time and space,
The other, a consulting detective, a man of the law.
It's an escape, a break.
But it's me, and that's what I love.

Megan Hall (15)
Kingswood Academy, Bransholme

Change

Life rotates,
Like the Earth around the sun.
The seasons change,
Like cake batter to a bun.
Change is difficult,
Like a maths equation you can't solve,
It feels like the phrase, 'the same', just dissolves.
Change is new, that's just how it is.
Like a new Coca-Cola;
It begins to fizz.
But when the bubbles disappear,
And the drink is ready; 'in gear',
The change does the same,
The change becomes clear.

Evelyn Taylor (12)
Kingswood Academy, Bransholme

My Life

Football's the place that feels like home,
I love music exceptionally,
I love to read and write,
Sometimes I think I can be a bit tight.
I wear glasses to read,
But I do have lots of speed.
School is alright,
But at least I am bright.
I get called Izzy,
And I tend to be busy.
I love to eat sweets on Christmas.
I am very crazy,
But at home, I get called lazy.

Isabelle Hargreaves (11)
Kingswood Academy, Bransholme

The Climb

N ever be afraid of anything
I remember my first climb at the age of five
S mall steps to growing big
H elping hands that guided my stride
I learnt that no mountain is too big, with
K indness and bravery in your heart
A nd that's my adventure of growing up.

Nishika Deodhar (11)
Kingswood Academy, Bransholme

For Sparks

Spark of joy in a fruitful life,
Climb together, let there be no strife.
Hold the flame, be its light,
Then burn away, and out of sight.

The fire falls dim,
But weak it is not.
Like filament so thin,
Just as it was wrought.

Spark of joy in a hollow life,
Heed the flame and all its rites.
Then be its refuge, home of cinder,
Until hope fuels hope, a free burning figure.

Yet, still cold you are,
You cry aid from afar.
So frozen joy, fading joy,
Build this ploy, be the decoy.

Our final spark, from what was once flame.
In a home of ash, for which only it can blame.

A hand alone, not cold, nor warm,
Alights our spark and again it is born.
Refuge eternal, under a comforting glow,
Calling hope, for the seeds it might sow.

From hand to spark once more,
Of joy in flame once more.
Given way to this new light,
Alleviated, it now takes flight.

So sparks, cry freely,
Together, cry freely.

Benjamin McEwan (16)
Lochgilphead High School, Lochgilphead

This Is Me

Hello, my name is Aladdine, and I am 12 years old,
And I was born in Italy in a beautiful and calm city,
In the countryside, called Prato.
I have three sisters;
Two are older than me and one is younger than me,
So I would be in the middle, I guess.
I had an amazing and wonderful community back in Prato,
I was always the fastest one at running,
And the best footballer in my year back in Italy,
But also, the wildest person in the whole school.
Unfortunately, I was very naughty,
Which resulted in me being referred to a psychologist,
And after that, a psychiatrist,
I knew I was not weird or naughty,
I just needed someone to listen to me,
Which was something I was deprived of in kindergarten.
I also used to get into many fights back in my school,
And I was also very cheeky, which affected my learning,
And that was the reason I had to repeat kindergarten.
I got sent to a youth centre,
For two hours and 30 minutes every single day,
Just to play and ride a bike.
And then came the summer,
Where I went swimming for the last time
Until I got bombed with the worst news ever,

And that was when I got the news
That I was going to move to England.
I was very sceptical at first about moving
Because I only had a few lessons in the English language
And I knew basic words like:
'Good', 'yes', 'good morning' and 'hello'
And I would have to leave all my friends,
Which was the saddest thing to do,
But when Mom said I was going to have a better life,
That is when I gave in.
A week later, I was on the plane going to England,
To a great and welcoming city called Manchester.
When we arrived, I was happy
That there was a youth centre right next to me,
And that is when I discovered reading,
And I was reading so much that I did not realise
The books were shaping me over the years,
And that is when I became the luckiest person;
As I was put into Loreto High School.
I had the chance to make friends again,
And even if I got bullied,
And called cringe, weirdo, loud, or strange,
I never let that stop me from becoming who I am today.
Today, I am an extraordinarily strong, confident and
Happy person and that is me, I am Aladdine Abed.

Aladdine Abed (12)
Loreto High School, Chorlton

Who Am I?

Can you tell me about you?
Your personalities?

I can answer it all.
But it will be a never-ending story like a rolling ball.

Who am I?
I am Bess and I came from Hong Kong,
The story will be long.

I have hazel brown eyes,
Like two tiny forests,
Covered in secrets.

Who am I?
A person who likes drawing,
By watching and thinking.
Thoughts blow into my mind,
And I start making an amazing design.

I also like reading,
You can call it an obsession.
Wherever I go,
A book of me will show.

Who am I?
I am a monkey,
Although I'm cranky,
I dance funkily.

Music makes me as cool as a cucumber,
It makes me feel like I'm living in another world,
Makes winter feel like summer.

I have a little sister,
She's captivated by fruits.
Sometimes annoying,
However, she is amazing.

It'd be a longer story,
If I didn't end it here.
As you read it clearly,
This is who I am,
And I like the way I am me.

Bess Lee (12)
Loreto High School, Chorlton

This Is Me

I have heard I could be a bird and fly away with glee,
Or speak as loud as a lion,
But the truth is no more than me,
Me is me and I is I,
Don't be ashamed about when you lied,
Speak out with glee, know there is a new start because,
Me is me and I is I, there is nothing more than I,
So, like I said, leave it behind,
Start with a new page in life,
Though people hit me, I get back up and say,
You will not stop me from doing what I love,
Drama is my love, and so are PE and music,
But I am proud of who I can be and what I am,
I have a disability, in S.E.N.D.
With dyslexia, it will never end,
Though people laugh at me,
It's a superpower in my life
Because me is me and I is I,
Nothing more than you,
Now, I have to say goodbye,
This is me and this is my life.

Eamon Wilcox (12)
Loreto High School, Chorlton

I Am Strong, I Am Passionate, I Am A Footballer

Football, a game so grand,
Where players on the field take a stand.
The roar of the crowd, the cheers so loud.
As they watch their team, make us proud.

The ball is kicked, it soars up high,
The players chase it, reaching for the sky.
With skill and strategy, they play the game,
Passing, shooting, aiming for fame.

So let's kick off and have some fun,
In this game that brings us all together as one.
Football, a sport that never gets old,
A beautiful story to be told.

Godswill Benjamin Aigbedo (11)
Loreto High School, Chorlton

This Is Me

Earthquakes, floods, wars and crimes,
Are items in these modern times.
But I am happy and as safe as can be,
As my family keep them away from me.
I go to school to learn every day,
And with my friends, socialise and play.
I like to learn, play and sing,
However, drama is my favourite thing.
An only child I may be,
But family means the world to me.
Nana, Grandad and Mum too,
We stick together as families do.

Megan Hardy (12)
Loreto High School, Chorlton

This Is Me

This is me, I am as free as a bee,
I think being free is for people like me.
I found my place, found my home,
But some are unlucky, trying to find their home.
And then it struck me, harder than lightning,
If you help them and make them feel safe, feel free
They will find their home.
This is who I am; a helper, a friend,
And if you need help finding your home
I will help you, never together, but never alone.

Alex Clarke (11)
Loreto High School, Chorlton

This Is Me

I am a kind and funny person,
With a heart that shines like a star.
I make everyone feel at ease,
And my laughter is like a gentle breeze.

My smile is like the sun,
And my jokes are always fun.
I have a way of making people smile,
And my kindness goes the extra mile.

I'm always there to lend a hand,
And I make this world a better land.
My heart is pure and full of love,
And I'm an angel sent from above.

Chace Brennan (13)
Loreto High School, Chorlton

This Is A Normal Day In My Normal Life

I wake up in the morning and have breakfast,
This is me.
My mum drives me to school,
This is me.
I go to breakfast club and meet my friends,
This is me.
I go to my lessons,
This is me.
I go to break,
This is me.
I say bye to my friends,
This is me.
I go home,
This is me.
I play with my friends,
This is me.
I go to bed,
This is me!

Malachy Doherty (11)
Loreto High School, Chorlton

This Is Me, I Am... Lucia!

I get anxious when it comes to speaking aloud,
I don't like being alone,
I'm shy,
I am helpful,
I get really confused when it comes to certain things,
All these things about me are true,
Yes, but that doesn't mean,
I can't be a good friend,
Or that I'm stupid or that I don't care,
This is just who I am.

Lucia Box (13)
Loreto High School, Chorlton

My Life

My life is quite crazy,
But at the same time, I am a bit lazy.
I love to sleep,
And have fun on the streets.
I go to Loreto High School,
I sadly get told off by swinging on the science stools.
My name is Hanna,
But I hate when people call me Hanna Banana.
I am good at gymnastics,
I also know my friends are fantastic!

Hanna Cassandra (12)
Loreto High School, Chorlton

B.R.O.D.I.E.

B rave and adventurous, never dangerous
R acing and bringing laughter
O vernight, bugs bite. Itching for days, trying to escape this maze
D eep underwater, in the middle of the year, it gets warmer
I n the game, trying to aim at the flame
E verton Football Club every week, hoping we win.

Brodie Johnson (11)
Loreto High School, Chorlton

Ezra

E nergetic, enthusiastic
Z ealously smiling, spreading joy
R eally, really respectful
A lways active.

Ezra Walker (11)
Loreto High School, Chorlton

This Is Me

I'm as wide awake as an owl,
Dark as the night, such a fright.
Through the dark gloom, I see a light,
My bedroom light shines so bright.
Sat pondering about the day,
Knowing the next day is only a few hours away.
As I look forward to the laughter on the car journey in,
There starts my day and I'm ready to begin.
My name is called, I'm focused and poised,
I open my book, pen in my hand,
Pen to paper words that demand.
English, science, it's all sinking in,
Numbers, equations; maths is just about to begin.
I'm now writing my story as my journey begins,
I will make history, but one day at a time.
I have passion, I have fire,
I look beyond my desires.
Beating, drumming, hopping around,
Listening to music, what a beautiful sound.
Sometimes my emotions cause some commotion,
Happy or sad, it doesn't last long,
Peaceful and calm, there's no cause for alarm.
For I am me and you are you, everyone's destiny awaits.
I shall wait for you at the gates with my mates.
Smiles on faces, we are going places.

Now, I must bring this poem to an end,
Because this has been driving me round the bend!
Now, it is all said and done,
I will make my departure and run!

Eva Johns (12)
Matford Brook Academy, Exeter

This Is Me

I'm just writing stuff that relates to me,
For other people to see,
But maybe I'm more than a person with a page and a pen.
Maybe I'm a kind, compassionate soul that likes science, as a whole!
Maybe I'm the kind of person you want to talk to, I'm thoughtful.
Maybe I'm the kind of kid who likes sports too.
This is a story,
All about me.
I've just started secondary,
Life is kind of hard for me,
While I'm adjusting to this new world I see.
But I try my hardest to be the best,
So this is the beginning of my story.

Ewan Dunlop (11)
Matford Brook Academy, Exeter

I Am A Boy

I am a boy
Although I was born a girl
Like a harp, my heartstrings are pulled towards the idea of total masculinity Everything in my mind is blue
But I am told to think pink
"Hey, ma'am!", "Hey, Lady!", "Hey, Girl!"
Who are you talking to?
That's not me.
Can't you see I'm a boy?
Can't you see?
My tears weep pink, the pastel, the hotness
But why are they not blue?
Why was I put down here to live in this cosy aroma
The sun, the trees, the dirt
Without a body to call mine?
Can't you see how I long for it?
Can't you see?
I am that masculine power
I am me.

Ed Constantine (15)
Melbury College - Lavender Campus, Mitcham

My Mask

We all have a mask that we put up when we are afraid,
mine is more often.
Our masks are not who we are, just a cover-up of the waves
of emotion crashing beneath them.
When our masks get too full of buckets of emotions, they
snap, shatter and break.
This is when the great tsunami of sensations, hormones and
lingering worries come rippling out.
Our worries, nerves and disturbances are often
unpredictable, pouncing at us like a vicious panther on its
weak prey, during the worst of times,
Almost like a huge slap in the face,
Although this one hurts mentally.

I often find myself trying my hardest to stitch my pieces
back together.
However, not even the strongest glue could fix an already
broken mask.
I tried everything to tame the wild flood from beneath.
Unfortunately, Sellotape was just not enough this time.
Scattered fragments from my defeated mask remained lost
within my mind.

Once my mask had finally given in,
My body and mind dwelled in its loss.
My cover had finally collapsed in, exposing my true self,
Which lay below piles upon piles of anxiety, distress and
concerns.

However, after a while, I came to the conclusion,
I no longer needed a mask at all.

Iggy Rinaldi (14)
Melbury College - Lavender Campus, Mitcham

My World, Your World

This is our world, we all belong to it.
Friends, family, environment, atmosphere,
What we learn and what we are taught,
Who we trust, who is there for us,
What we know,
Our ideas, our opinions,
Our dislikes and likes,
Our experiences and how we are raised,
Our heritage and culture,
What we look like and how we are treated.
These are the things that shape us,
These are the things that create our personalities,
These are the things we should be proud of.
No matter who we are,
What we look like,
There should be equality.
This is our world, we all belong to it.
Therefore, in this world, we must be equal.
To be equal means:
To have the chance to be judged fairly,
To have the chance for justice,
To stand trial for what you have done,
And not what you haven't,
To look at the proof that is given,
And not where you come from or how you talk,

To make up ideas as we get to know a person,
And not to judge a book by its cover,
Because everyone is different,
Yet we are all so similar.
We have all grown up in the same world,
And we need to look after it,
Because this is our world, we all belong to it.

Mia Thompson (14)
Melbury College - Lavender Campus, Mitcham

My Dilemma

Tackling the truths which haunt our youths,
Too consumed by wasted potential,

Wanting to learn despite being warned,
Willing to navigate the misinformed,

But faced with questions -
Bombarded with misjudgement,

Flawed in their understanding,
Foraging for unfound reasoning,

A quest unending -
A cosmic search in the making,

Trusting yourself is essential.
These final words are intentional.

Jessica Bame (14)
Melbury College - Lavender Campus, Mitcham

Am I Not?

I'm swallowed by the darkness
So don't try and tell me that
I'm sitting in the light now
My friends don't care
It's false to say that
I have no right to feel sad, crazy or mad
No, I don't have to fake a smile
I'm reminded every day that
I'm too broken to receive the help that may save me
And nothing you say will challenge me to believe that
I deserve love in any form
No matter if I had been chosen to be born as
I am no longer worth the heartaches
Even if my own heart should break
And I can't assume why you shall think it's true that
I'm swallowed by the darkness
So don't tell me to believe
I'm bright and creative
I know myself better than you
So, the debate is so
Am I really alone?

(Now read from the bottom to the top)

Taylor Jade Smith (12)
Middlewich High School, Middlewich

I Am...

I am a girl
I am a woman

I am a child of a broken home
I am a child of four

I am a girl with a copy
I am a woman of so many

I am a child who lives
I am a child from fantasy

I am a girl who loves men
I am a woman who loves women

I am a child with joy
I am a child with fear

I am a girl from a small town
I am a woman with big dreams

I am a child of wind and water
I am a child of earth and fire

I am a girl of pride
I am a woman of love

I am a child of this Earth
I am a child of love

I am all of these things
I am human
I am me.

Ava Hulbert-Thompson (14)
Middlewich High School, Middlewich

This Is Me...

This is me, a daughter, an awesome author,
A singer who listens to music most of you wouldn't sing along to,
A netballer, a crier, a fighter, a food eater,
A big believer, a best friend, a leader, a player,
A person with big dreams, an evolution believer,
A non-sleeper, a hard worker, a box collector,
A football lover, an enthusiastic reader, a Henry VIII wives liker,
A movie watcher, a weight lifter, a science lover, a super sister, a dancer, me.
This is me!

Kayley Rostron (11)
Middlewich High School, Middlewich

This Is Me

This is me,
People say I am weak,
I am too small,
I am ugly.

But I don't listen,
I know who I am,
I am strong,
I am brave,
I am beautiful.

I rise above it,
I am me,
And I wouldn't change anything.

I am the pop songs I listen to,
I am love and happiness.

This is me.

Freya Smith (12)
Middlewich High School, Middlewich

The New Life

This is me,
Running as fast as the speed of sound
Towards the new world,
The new life, don't look at my fears or my worries,
Look at me, not what I pretend to be, just simply see
Me
See my dreams, my accomplishments and my hopes,
Not what you wish for me,
Just look at me,
I'm here
This is me, this is all I can be
And what I'll always be.

Charlie Sedgwick (11)
Middlewich High School, Middlewich

This Is Me: I Am

I am swinging through the vines of a dark, mysterious forest with courage.
I am swimming in the deepest, darkest waters with strength.
I am at home with my family relaxing with happiness.

This is me: I am anxious, happy, lonely, nice, smiley, adventurous.
This is me: I am whatever I want to be and nobody can stop me.

Natasha Fox
Middlewich High School, Middlewich

This Is Me

I can be brave,
I can be strong,
I can be smart,
I can belong.

I can be afraid,
I can be shy,
I can be nervous,
I can be upset and not know why.

But I can, I am kind,
I am caring,
I am funny,
And I am me.

This is me,
And that's all I'll ever be.

Emelia Marlow-Ellis (12)
Middlewich High School, Middlewich

Butterfly

Butterfly, o butterfly,
Please don't fly away,
Your fragile wings light up my day,
O your colours are so beautiful,
You bring joy and happiness,
I can't wait till next summer,
So I can see your beautiful colours again.

Jessica Helm
Middlewich High School, Middlewich

This Is Me

This is me,
A sea of creativity,
An ocean, calm and serene,
Rippling with happiness and shoals of feelings.
My sparkling waves are unique,
But surge against barriers,
Always determined.

This is me,
My waves creeping up to the shore,
Slowly but steadily achieving my goals,
Sucking up grains of encouragement as I go.
Even if my waters recede from the land,
I can trickle back again,
Always persevering.

This is me,
Coral reefs of freedom,
Life thrives in my seas of courage.
Tsunamis of kindness,
Endless exploration,
Always there for others.

This is me,
Wild and free.

Always just proud to be,
This is me.

Darley-Rose Fryatt (11)

Moyles Court School, Ringwood

This Is Me

Dance:
Dancing is my passion,
I love to dance to the beat of the music,
And feel free to move how I like,
And have no particular way to do it.

Fashion:
Fashion is key in life,
Everything must go,
I love to dress the way I feel,
Your style tells a lot about a person.

Make-up:
I consider myself a make-up artist,
Make-up is like my canvas,
I try new things, new colours,
And new shapes on my face,
My face is a canvas to me.

I am a lazy person,
Who likes all of these things.
I like to try new things.
I am also a magical wizard,
I went to Hogwarts.
I am so powerful.
So yeah, this is me.

Tommy Knight (11)
Moyles Court School, Ringwood

This Is Me: Yisaac Yuen

She's the one I trust the most
Always there when I'm alone
Not a day goes by when she's not by my side
Every day that goes by,
The feeling makes us closer, like time
We met in September but she's always on my mind

You never seem to judge me
Or ever let me down
You put a smile on my face
Whenever you see a frown

You're better than a sister
You're more than just a girlfriend
You have a special place in my heart
That's why you're my best friend

Trust is earned
Respect is given, and
Loyalty is demonstrated.
Betrayal to any one of these,
Is to lose all three.

Yisaac Yuen (12)
Moyles Court School, Ringwood

Netball

Netball is just like life, really
When people watch, they think it's easy

You need a team to play it
Just like life, you can't do it on your own
It's like they act as a protective dome

Every day I grow a little bit stronger and a little bit better
A little bit faster, a little bit prouder
A bit more confident, a little happier!

Every day brings something new
So bring it on
Every challenge, every wall
I'll knock it down
Every word, every way
I'll say it louder and prouder
This is me!

Lorelei Lugg
Moyles Court School, Ringwood

This Is Me

This is me, I am interesting and energetic,
My fave sports are swimming and dance,
I find them epic.
This is me!

This is my destiny,
My eternity,
And my desire to be.
This is me!

I am an extrovert and kind,
I am positive and small,
And all good vibes combined.
This is me!

I am smart but I can get things wrong,
I will be who I want...
I will fight,
I will struggle,
I will win,
I will be what I want to be,
There is no stopping,
This is me!

Emilia Jackson
Moyles Court School, Ringwood

This Is Me

My favourite animal brings me peace,
And reassures me that everything will be okay.

C aring and creative
A ffectionate and affable
P assionate and peaceful
Y oung and yielding
B eautiful and brilliant
A wesome and inspiring
R espectful and relaxed
A dmirable and accomplished.

But a lot of people don't know the grief,
I hold in from my dad dying.

This is me.

Arthur Ingham
Moyles Court School, Ringwood

Books

Books are amazing, books can take
You into another world in your mind
You can make it your own.

I just love books, they are superb,
There is nothing better. When I
Read, it makes me feel so happy.

It can take you anywhere you
Want, you can visit a fantasy land or
A crime scene or a manga world...

So, it is a gigantic world out there
For everyone, thanks to books
Which take you there.

Ben Lacey
Moyles Court School, Ringwood

This Is Me

Haiku poetry

On the court, I stand,
Netball passion fills my soul,
Determined and strong.

Through aisles, I roam free,
Shopping in my hands, I find,
Treasures to call mine.

Kindness in my heart,
Spreading love with every word,
Brightening each day.

Positive mindset,
Embracing life's joyful path,
Radiant and free.

Imogen Hordle
Moyles Court School, Ringwood

This Is Me

A n acrostic poem
C an be written about anything
R eally
O f course, some people tend to
S tart each line as a sentence
T hough
I like to make words into a
C reation that is more freehand...

Because this is me.

Chloe Beaumont (12)
Moyles Court School, Ringwood

Happiness

H appiness for everyone all around the globe
A ll to have kindness for everyone, no matter what
P ositivity shown to everyone of every ethnicity and social group
P eace and love to be spread across every country
I magining a world full of joy and affection
N o neglect to anyone in any situation
E quality between all races, countries and nationalities
S ympathy for all who need it at any moment in time
S atisfaction for everyone to be living in a kind, joyful and equal society.

Courtney Smith
Netherthorpe School, Staveley

How The World Sees Me

I wish I could change how the world sees me,
Not as a missing puzzle piece,
Or as some wild rampaging beast,
I wish I could be seen as the real me...

Through my windows, you would see
A vision of creativity.
Please, I really don't want your sympathy,
Even with this 'missing piece' in me.

Embrace my uniqueness, let me be me,
My beautiful colours, they're shining through,
And see me beyond the 'puzzle view',
I'm still so young, so let me be free.

You think I'm a girl who's always in trouble,
That I don't listen, yet I hear every word.
You say I'm like a trapped little bird,
A person who lives in an 'autistic bubble'.

I wish I could change how the world sees me,
A kaleidoscope of thoughts and dreams,
A symphony of minds bursting through the seams,
I knew I was different since I was three.

I'll dance to a rhythm only I can hear,
The loud noises are scary,
And I don't like hands that are sweaty,
But I navigate a world, that seems so unclear.

I wish the world could change how it sees me,
So I don't have to change myself.

Bryony Roberts
Nicholas Chamberlaine School, Bedworth

This Is Me

This is me
I am really funny
I love football
And I wish to be tall
Mathematics, my favourite subject
In Year 9, it is what I wish to study
My secondary school is North Birmingham Academy
A school that makes people feel like a big family
A kind and smart person is who I am
And I really want to be in Buckingham
Home of the King's palace
Hopefully, I can get a pass
I am a really friendly man
Who loves Batman
This is all about me
And I am Tirmidhi.

Tirmidhi Adedeji
North Birmingham Academy, Erdington

This Is Me

This is me
A humble being on Planet Earth
Not a bee
Not a tree
A human being since birth.
Nothing makes me different
Not who I love
Or what I look like
Just my personality
Not if I can ride a bike
All I ask for is my life.

This is me
I love music and dancing
Singing and pranking.
Let me be
This is me.

Aine Shirley
North Birmingham Academy, Erdington

This Is Me

I am me
I am unique
I might be broken
I might be fixed
I am beautiful, happy and joyful
I am mixed race; half-Asian, half-white
I have brown hair, I have a different style
I don't like bugs but I like mud
I am not a girly girl, I am a tomboy
I haven't really got it figured out yet
But I still love me.
I am me!

Asrah Jackson
North Birmingham Academy, Erdington

This Is Me

This is me, I am me,
Proud and kind.
My favourite colour is green,
And I have two cats.
I am proud of myself for who I am,
And I am never ever gonna change.
I am unique and nobody
Will make me change myself.

Selma Haddouche
North Birmingham Academy, Erdington

This Is Me

This is me, full of glee
I am so humane
Brighter than a tree
I live
I love
I laugh
This is me
A joyful, adventurous, short being
Happy is my most common feeling
So, this is me!

Gunjan Lal
North Birmingham Academy, Erdington

Me, Myself And I

Me, Myself and I
My three reliable cards
My three different angles
Slowly turning into alter egos
Each of them double-sided
Ready to play at any time.

Each card a different weakness
A different side
A different job
A different strength.

Me, the intelligent and determined card
Ready to be used
When there is a challenge, of course
Nothing can stop me.

Then there is the other side of me
Obsessed with the word 'success'
Once I've started, I become addicted.

Have to finish it, you can do it!
Don't embarrass yourself!
Don't say the words!
Don't say you can't do it...
People will think you're weak.

Then there is Myself, the child
The confused part of myself
Seeking answers
Entering new stages of my life
Secondary school, growing
A new chapter, a completely new world.

Emotional, a word frequently used to describe me
Being emotional can be a good thing
I can connect with people faster
Understand them when other people don't,
A different power
I know what people want, how to please them.

Sometimes I go too far
I become too devoted
Who I know can't let go of me
Turn into a shoulder to cry on for others, a reusable tissue
I don't know how to say *no*
I take my feelings out on others
Am I the Joker in my set of cards?

I, the best side of me
The extroverted side
The side I normally show to others
My confidence is brought to light
My friends, my family, a weapon

My strengths playing their part
No haters, no worries.

This side makes me a people-pleaser
But why do I care so much about their opinions?
Just stop caring, why can't you stop?
Everybody turns into critics
Calm down, they will forget
But when will I forget?

This is me
A confused girl in a chaotic world
On a path of self-discovery
Left on a cliff-hanger each day
With the questions
What will happen next?
When will my three cards become one?

Ayesha Alim (11)
Northampton School For Girls, Spinney Hill

Promises To The Next

A life that I wish to forget.
A fake self that I created,
To fit in around the ones that can.
A life where I know the language of the ones before me;
Instead of not being able to talk in my mother's tongue like my ancestors.
Talking in a foreign language in a foreign land.

I remember taking out the braids that my mother so carefully weaved in,
So I wouldn't be a target for the teasing that continued in my primary days.
How I wished to have long blonde hair that flowed just perfectly.
How I wished to be one that had it.

But that doesn't happen in the foreign land, my dear.
You would always be the black sheep, be the one who is forever different.
For life put you there for a reason,
Yet the reason has already passed?
These are the words of promises to the next.

Keep your head high, don't live with sorrow or regret.
Laugh, cry, be strong.
Be who you were born to become;
Be the one that can hold the memories of ones who can't.

Dagan Abdillahi (13)
Northampton School For Girls, Spinney Hill

The Exception

Wistfully reconstructing the features,
Echoing upon broken mirror pieces,
Shattered across, limitlessly down,
With the intimacy of a fair-weather friend,
To whom the ground meant less of a reflection,
And more of an acknowledgement that I,
Would never be the exception.

As my eyes waver through the imitation,
Desperately searching for a sign that I,
Would be the exception.

Expectantly catching a glimpse of artistry,
Weaving into colours in, out and between,
Each spool of string unravelling galore,
Meeting their ends and encompassing themselves,
Onto the floor as succumbed threads apart,
Torn away from each other, no longer as one,
Gradually encasing me into a cast,

Transitioning from the cloaking of my toes,
To the choking of my throat,
The words weakly orchestrated out,
In a scheme of high-noted shrills to muffled begs.
And with the loss of an unsharpened weapon,

Bruises and cuts tattooed onto my skin, left their mark proudly,
Knowing this was for the aspiration of being the exception.

Tolerating the slashes scratched into my unkempt fingers and ego,
The supple stature of pencils was held gingerly,
Further willing to leave a mark on a canvas
Other than my own, yet sharing a similar dose of naivety
Filling every imaginable shade to every laid-out barrier,
The dyed graphites rebelliously found themselves unwinding their way out,
To complete all that was not meant to be,

And ultimately ripping the canvas, destructing it to plasters for I,
For whose wounds of any kind could never be healed.

Blinded from the boiling blood gurging out and,
Drenched in the lineage of my life, I was less alarmed,
And more accepting of the realisation that I,
Would never be the exception.

Hunsil Taseer Bhatt (15)
Northampton School For Girls, Spinney Hill

I Am Living

I am a dead land and dried up Earth,
Sink your fingers into the deep cracks,
Pull apart my layers with such glee,
Find the sweet nectar flowing beneath.
Drink me in.

Warm blood drips from your lips full of mirth,
I am the blood and the bone gone slack,
I am the muscles that propel me;
Into your arms.

Though, I am also the canvas now.
This stretched pale skin over wooden frame,
Paint that will tell a story for me always;
Stretch marks are pulled from my arms and nerves,
And scars that faintly trace memories.
Hang me up on your wall.

I am the wall too, the home somehow.
I'll fill bellies with warm food and love,
Your great joy echoes down my hallways,
Sit close to my heart, this fire burns.
I'll light your way home.

Both guide and follower, close to light.
I am a moth's wing that's fluttering at your side,
I'll be strong, I promise, uplifting you into the skies,

A glass bullet which impacts you,
With chubby fingers, you grasp me,
Ready to tear me in two.

A child I was, or that I still am?
My skin is warm with the blood of my family,
My skin is warm from my mother's hands,
I'll rest my head against her bosom with her heart as my own.
It's warm like my father's laugh, which trembles in my throat.
I am both my father and my mother,
Their faces are reflected in every mirror.
Forgive me for what I could not be.

I am everything, a life experiencing itself in human form.
I am the space that I take up,
A glowing in my chest,
The ache in your bones,
I am the mountains and stones,
All that is unknown.
I am alive.

I am living.

Edie Walker (17)
Northampton School For Girls, Spinney Hill

I Am Human

I am human,
I am child,
I am youth.
I observe from a distance and hear the others scream:
"We are the saviours of this rotting Earth!"
"We are the new generation!"
We are *human.*
They do not speak for me.
I am no saviour.
I was born, and I will die, alone.
I am living for myself and myself only.

I am human,
I am black,
I am beautiful.
To some, I was born a queen.
To others, another loud-mouthed little girl to patronise and control.
I am the image of equality, not to be confused with the white man, of course.
Everybody knows that all white men are the symbol of greed and bigotry, right?
Wrong.
But who am I to tell the difference?

I am human,
I am grown,

I am free
From the confines of mandatory education,
Restricting my creative flow
And filling my young mind with stressful expectations
In preparation for the adult world.
"I don't need school to be successful!"
Because I know I'd fail anyway.

I am human,
I am weak,
I am "slave to the system".
But only when this society's government doesn't feel like aiding a generation of rebels.
Raised by the internet, my brain developed faster than my body.
Only now am I beginning to face the consequences of having a childhood.

I am human,
I am poetic,
I am aware of what happens around me.
I know I am not beautiful enough for the standard here.
I know I am not intelligent enough to be recognised.
I know I am not vocal enough to stand for what I believe in.
But this lack of speciality is what makes me *human.*

Yannick Chidumo (13)
Northampton School For Girls, Spinney Hill

Father Of The Year

My first heartbreak wasn't a boy in the playground,
Not even my first boyfriend,
It was the first man I have ever loved,
The man who used to read me bedtime stories,
The man meant to mend all my broken hearts,
It was my father,
The first man every little girl loves.

However, my father wasn't the man he so claimed to be,
He broke my heart into tiny little pieces,
Leaving me to pick them up all alone,
Shards of my heart stuck into my fingers,
I carry on into the unknown.

Life without my father,
The worst thought at best,
My mother held me most nights,
I held myself the rest.

I cry for my younger self at night,
For all she wanted was her father to love her,
A father to be proud of her,
A father to care for her.

I have always been told: "At least you have a dad."
"You're just being dramatic."
"It can't be that bad."

Yes, he may have been physically present,
But deep down, he was emotionally absent.

Where were you, Dad?
Where were you when I needed you the most?
Where were you when I took my first step?
I will never know,
Because you were never there,
And you never will be.

All I wanted was one hug,
One kind word,
One token of affection,
All I needed was your love.

I shouldn't have to ask you to be a father to me,
You are the reason I cannot love or trust so easily,
In the end, we will never be the same,
We will never be able to fix the heart you once broke,
I guess this is how we were always meant to be,
Our relationship, nothing but a joke.

Autumn Houghton (13)
Northampton School For Girls, Spinney Hill

A Memory

Who am I?

Just a girl, one of many
More specifically, a pale girl with blonde hair
But since when did my looks make me, myself?
For I am just a face
Made up of generations before me.

Then, who am I?
Am I just the awkward, strange girl
Who enjoys games and reading?
But is it really me?

Am I someone who carries the blood
Of a powerful flag
With meaningful colours
That has been burned into
A once glorious memory?

Or am I flesh and bones
With each nerve working together
To send electrical signals to my brain?

Am I going to be a powerful, significant figure
That will carry the opinion and voice
Strong enough to save lives?

Or will I just be another girl
Whose name will slowly rust away
Only to be remembered by files
Carrying dust in a filing cabinet.

I await Fate's dark ink
To write down my path
Determining my every choice
My every mistake
Then maybe I'll know who I will be.

Or maybe I will be just a memory
For people to remember
As my body is rested

Upon an earthly womb
Never to be seen again

But for now, I'm just a girl.

Rebeka Stonkus (15)
Northampton School For Girls, Spinney Hill

Sins

"First angel up," called the young Baptist,
His voice rested, not raising it the slightest,
Aurora stepped forward, her heart filled with joy,
This would be the day her sins would no longer be wrong,
Pale blue roses lined the pool,
This made Aurora feel fresh and cool,
With a calm touch, the Baptist grabbed her hand,
As their eyes met for one final glance.
Her heart thumped faster and faster,
Leaving her mind just to become a dancer.
Her hands sweated like crazy,
Only for her words to come out all wavy.
"Don't let me go," Aurora cried,
As she pulled the Baptist deep inside.
Their bodies clasped together,
While the water wrapped them tight,
Her white flowy dress was soon out of sight,
No colours except nude and light.
"Let's stay like this forever and ever,
No one can separate us,
For that will only make them dread us."
The sound on the outside faded away,
But alas, Aurora disappeared all the same.
"Fly away, you evil raven,
For I am not the dove you should be craving."

All sins are non-existent in holy water,
But do they ever come back?

Samantha George (11)
Northampton School For Girls, Spinney Hill

My Life

This is me,
Thinking about the future.
This was me,
Thinking of today.

Now, I don't know what will come,
But one thing is for sure.
Every day comes with a new adventure,
A new page in a book,
A new end of the day.

But you will never know what is next,
That's why we are here to twist and turn around every corner,
To see what comes next.
That's why I'm stuck on this journey of jump scares,
And a variety of emotions.

That is me,
A curious girl,
I can't stop thinking about what will come,
What is next?
What will today's suspense be?
When will the adventure end?
What will I see today?

This is me,
A fearless girl,
Ready for any moment to cry,
Always on edge,
Never ready to give up,
Never ready to end the story,
This is me.

A normal girl waiting for a new opportunity to come,
Waiting for a cliffhanger,
Awaiting a new page,
Never wanting to end the story.

This is me,
Thinking of the future.
That was me,
Thinking of today.

Nicole Chiritoi (11)
Northampton School For Girls, Spinney Hill

Mosaic

I'm a mosaic, a tapestry woven
Out of all the people I've ever loved.
You would find, if you cut me in half,
That I am my best friend's contagious laugh.
Beautifully flawed are the pieces we share -
I run my fingers along the seams.
How magnificent it feels to be sewn together
By all those who have laid their souls bare.

I'm a painting, a work of art;
Every brushstroke is a breath, a whisper of souls
Whose paths intertwined with mine long ago.
I am my mother's pain, I am my father's grief,
I am the tears my brother shed
When he grazed his knees and it seeped
A violent, unforgiving red.
Through me, their symphonies are passed on,
Even after they're gone.

I'm a galaxy, a constellation
Crafted from the crevices of their hearts.
I am the light they've shown me.
I am the blurred lines between souls.
But tell me, my dear, where do you end?
Where do I begin?

On nights like these,
I look at my face in the mirror.
I am my own ghost.

Alina Irfan (16)
Northampton School For Girls, Spinney Hill

Mirror, Mirror

Mirror, mirror, *who am I?*
Am I courageous or am I shy?
Am I loyal or am I sly?
Do I find joy or do I cry?

Mirror, mirror, *who am I?*
Am I tall or am I short?
When I chortle, do I snort?
Do you think that I like sport?

Mirror, mirror, *who am I?*
Am I nerdy or just curious?
What current affairs make me furious?
What do I relish in or find humorous?

Mirror, mirror, *who am I?*
What's my biggest hope and dream?
How strong is my self-esteem?
What colour are my eyes, are they green?

Mirror, mirror, I am strong,
I am loyal and abhor playing sport,
I find joy in puzzles and I'm glum if I fail,
I'm cute and snort when I laugh!

Mirror, mirror, I am curious,
And lots of things make me furious,
I love books and find jokes humorous,
My biggest dream is to play Quidditch!

Mirror, mirror, I am me!

Evie Bennett (15)
Northampton School For Girls, Spinney Hill

This Is Me: I Am... You

My name is made up, my hobbies, my youth,
I am not me but I am you,
This version of me is a deception of truth,
I am not me, I am you.

Your empty standards craft and sculpt me,
I'm lost in a labyrinth of lies,
I hide in the back but wish for the glee,
I'm pathetic, with tears in my eyes.

Every day repeats itself over and over again,
Just existing is not living,
They tell me to pretend.

Thick layers of make-up mask my expression,
I realise how cruel they are,
They don't want my opinions but my possessions,
I will not let them leave a scar.

One day, I'll be me, not you,
With personal interests and thoughts,
I'll cut my hair and dye it too,
But till then, I'll be trapped in quartz.

My name is _____ , you can call me strange,
But I know who I am now.
This is me, and I won't change,
You cannot tear me down.

Amanda Bajan (14)
Northampton School For Girls, Spinney Hill

I Am Meant To Be Me

I am not like anyone else, I am different

And that isn't a problem at all
Mia is my name and that is what I'm called

Many wouldn't realise others' hidden talents
Even their own
And most of the time, they don't recognise mine
Now, I can express who I am meant to be - me - I never stay in the lines
Tomorrow is just another day for me to strive to accomplish - and I will - something, at least

Today, I achieved many goals - finishing this poem being one of them
Over and over, the days will bring new challenges for me to turn into goals - ones I shall achieve

Being young and being me is who I am meant to be
Endlessly, I shall be me, myself or I - it will never change

Mia is my name and that is what I'm called
Endlessly, I shall be me.

Mia Riviere (11)
Northampton School For Girls, Spinney Hill

The Smile That Changed

The pleasures are different to what they used to be,
The people I now see,
The languages I can speak,
The happiness I can now leak.

The best friends,
The trends,
Are still so real,
But I can't help but love the deal.

We set on each other,
But can't help the other,
Get bigger and bigger,
As your enemy starts to snigger.

Your happiness now cannot suffice,
The thoughts that you can't put upon a price,
And the new things that will shine through,
That put the worried things you thought you knew.

And behind the glass,
You smile and laugh,
At the new enjoyments you can play,
Now nothing can lead me astray.

In the sport that I love,
The country I love,
The animal I love,
The besties I love,

And the family that I love.

Scarlett Walton (12)
Northampton School For Girls, Spinney Hill

I Bruise Like A Peach

Sometimes I feel as if I am not quite ripe,
Like my skin is too green and my flesh is far too flavourless.
Often I am a peach,
Bruised beneath the eyes,
Bruises that are romanticised.
They are compared carelessly to fields of lilacs ready
to be plucked,
Compared to beauty.
But oh how I wish to be an orange.
Hidden beneath that blanket of protection,
Always at an arm's length of anybody's affection.
They dazzle in their amber-coloured spotlight,
They dazzle as they are peeled and rived.
But I am a peach,
And I do not dazzle,
I bruise.
I bruise as each healthy hand is given a chance to know me.
To peel me.
Yet, I go black and blue.
Why can't I taste like citrus, like the others do?

Bonnie Scoles (15)
Northampton School For Girls, Spinney Hill

The Words I'll Forget By Tomorrow

My mouth clamped shut,
The words that struggle free are smudged and slurred
My mind, an angsty cyclone,
Swirling with similes I'll forget by tomorrow
I try so hard to tell the world what I'm feeling,
The words I'm forgetting
Scrawled, misspelt on crumpled paper
But I'm afraid I have said too much or too little
I'll stare at this later and try to remember
The words I'll forget by tomorrow
My heart thumping,
The cyclone spiralling,
I desperately cling to elusive phrases
If only my emotions were to pour out
And splatter like ink on cream paper,
Forming sentences of perfect symphonies.

Haiqa Bhatt
Northampton School For Girls, Spinney Hill

My Past, My Present, My Future

I am the past.
I was colourful,
I was bright,
and I was young.
I was naive.
I am the past.

I am the present.
Littered with sadness and insecurity;
But hardened with reality.
I am patient and forgiving.
I have aged and changed,
But not lost who I was.
I am the present.

I am the future.
I will wrinkle, break and be broken,
Crackle and repair.
I will adapt and morph to my heart's desire;
Even when it grows weak.
I will crave for the past,
Where I had not been marked with age,
Or riddled with despair.

I will remake myself until,
I will be fractured and fragmented beyond repair.
I am the future.

Lesley Teal (15)
Northampton School For Girls, Spinney Hill

I Am Unique

This is me. I am a...

S mart
T alented
U nique individual
D etermined
E xtraordinary
N ever give up
T ill the end.

I am...

I am unique,
I like to go above and beyond the expectations,
Uniqueness sparks individuality,
I like to be different,
I am unique.

I am dedicated,
I work hard each day,
I always strive for the very best,
I love what I do and rush for success,
I am unique.

I am intelligent and smart,
I want to explore the world and increase my knowledge,
Because I am dedicated about learning till the end,

I am dedicated and devoted,
I am unique.

Aiza Haseeb (13)
Northampton School For Girls, Spinney Hill

Trying

I am trying,
I am trying to write.
To hold my pen with a grip so strong,
That my words are filled with might.

I am trying,
I am trying to shout.
To free my trapped words,
And let my mind pry out.

I am trying,
I am trying to be.
To exist and flourish,
Or at least to a certain degree.

I am trying,
I am trying to let go.
To move on from my mistakes,
But there are some things I wish I didn't know.

I am trying,
I am trying to grow.
To learn how to write, shout,
How to be and let go.

I am trying.

And that is all I know.

Bethany Rogers (14)
Northampton School For Girls, Spinney Hill

2015

2015, primary school was a breeze,
Never had a voice amongst the voices
Yet coming home, I was never at ease
Being the youngest - I had no choices.
House not a home, like a wilting flower
I was tainted with an inner stigma,
Dusk roses sat sitting in the shower
I'd search the stars - what an enigma.
I'm reminiscing about the relatable
Let's cease the round, the trend, the tradition
I'm reminiscing about the debatable
And I'm moving, like a smooth transition.
I thought the rings were for us to see
Yet in 2023 - I am free.

Brightrose Maphosa (16)
Northampton School For Girls, Spinney Hill

I Am Just One Average Little Girl

I am an average person, just like you,
Just an ordinary person living life to its fullest,
Oh, but I wish I only knew,
Why my personality switches.

I am an average girl,
An average girl who believed everything,
An average girl who just believed in her dreams,
An average girl who couldn't escape reality.

I am an average girl who likes art and music,
Just like any other average girl would,
A girl who would love to perform in public,
Either on stage or in the woods.

This is who I am,
Just one average little girl.

Ridhima Ganguly (13)
Northampton School For Girls, Spinney Hill

I Will Change The World

I am a doll in a doll shop on the windowsill.
I thought that everyone was different,
But I am the only different doll.
I just wait, wait, wait and wait.
Thinking, *what happened to all the colours and joy?*
While still never being picked.
Maybe I am the one who needs to change.
Maybe the world is not as different as I thought.
But no...
Maybe the world is what needs to change.
Maybe the world is not ready for me but I am ready for it.
I will change the world and all the people,
Because why do I have to change?

Sibylla Owens (12)
Northampton School For Girls, Spinney Hill

This Is Me

My walls are strong and powerful.
These colourful bricks that build me up,
Are mighty and capable.
I take shelter under my friends,
And my friends take shelter under me.
I have a base of honesty and kindness,
Topped with enthusiasm and craziness.
At my core, you will find my heart,
It's full of love and a passion for art.
I am made of confidence and consideration,
I am myself and... *This is me!*

Khushi Patel (11)
Northampton School For Girls, Spinney Hill

I Am Me

I am helpful, I am kind,
I wipe others' tears and listen to their cries,
The therapist friend, I listen, don't talk,
I never feel smart, only just a dork,
I put my feelings aside for others,
Thoughts and feelings all get smothered,
You probably wouldn't know,
As a fake smile is usually on show,
I can hide and I can fake,
But sometimes I break,
I am me.

Abigail Shiells (11)
Northampton School For Girls, Spinney Hill

Evolution Of A Picture

I pick up the sketchbook,
I feel the grain of the paper slipping through my fingers,
Rustling as I turn them,
I find a blank page crying out to be filled - to be blank no more.
I fumble for a pencil;
Its long slender form feels natural resting in my hand.
I draw the very first stroke on the page,
I feel joy in doing so.
A tidal wave of imagination flows through me,
Ideas overflow on the page; I'm unable to contain any more,
The sounds of the pencil gently scratching the paper resonates through the air.
The pencil dances across the page as if it has a mind of its own,
I feel calm as I work,
A world away from any worries.
Creativity courses through my fingers and pours onto the page;
A picture starts forming in the graphite scribbles.
I draw the last details,
Finally, it is complete.
I gaze at my piece.
I rest my pencil upon the surface - its job is done.
I am proud of my creation.

Tilly Wilkinson (13)
Northleigh House School, Hatton

This Is Me

I like hamsters and music,
I enjoy writing stories about my dreams before bed,
I'd be a writer if I could.
I love being alone,
But sometimes I hate it.
I have friends who I love to be around,
It makes me happy when I'm with them,
And I always have a big smile on my face.
My favourite movie is The School for Good and Evil.
I'm a very sensitive person,
And I have feelings that I sometimes bottle up.
I love being outside and exploring with my friends,
Laughing, gossiping; it makes me feel alive.
My favourite animals are hamsters,
I'd like to say that we're friends.
I talk to my best friend, Chelsee,
About practically everything.
Last year, my cousin moved to Australia,
I'll never recover from that.
I have a Staffy, fish and two hamsters,
Who I love very much.
You may find these things weird,
But this is me.

Kelsie Deville (11)
The Bolsover School, Bolsover

Who Am I?

I'm 14.
Or at least, I'm going to be.
I'm supposed to know everything,
I know nothing.
A century ago,
I could have been married,
But I can't even cook an egg right.
The world is confusing,
And constantly spinning.
Everything all the time.
I need a purpose in life,
But I feel useless.
I can't eat too much,
But I must love my body,
Whatever shape I end up being.
I need to embrace who I am,
But not stand out.
There is so much to buy.
And if I don't, I'm not 'cool', they will say.
But if I think my own thoughts,
I'd be cancelled for sure.
I walk the halls of the building,
The manufacturing ground,
The breeding unit.
We know it as school.

I wonder,
Am I just a number?
One tagged cow in a field of cattle,
Only valued by the price of my flesh.
Stuck in an endless churn
Of drones measured by convoluted stats.
Where are the parts of me,
That make life a lifetime?
Where are the lessons,
On finding happiness in capitalism?
Am I destined to be calculated,
By what output I provide,
By percentages submitted?
To be compared black and white.
Each day that goes by,
A part of me left behind.
Who even am I?

Zara Dudey (14)
The Bolsover School, Bolsover

This Is Me

Personality:
Shy, sensitive and kind,
I always try to be the best I can be.

Family:
A brother, stepbrother, stepsister, Dad, Mum, Step-mum, two dogs, one cat, one hamster, an aunty who owns seven dogs, two uncles, two grandads, Nana who owns a dog, Mamar who owns a dog, another aunty and five cousins.

Things I like:
My bed,
My phone,
My pets,
My family,
My friends,
My hair,
Art,
Food.

Things I don't like:
Spiders,
Birds,
People that bully,
Fake friends,
Waking up,
Spots,

Bugs,
Not having any classes with my best friend.

Things I love to do:
Go on my phone,
Be organised,
Midnight walks,
Go to Alton Towers,
Go to the park,
Call.

Things I love about me:
I try my hardest at school,
I'm honest,
I'm grateful,
Mostly everything.

Maisie Pope (11)
The Bolsover School, Bolsover

My Family

So not everything is up to par at the minute,
I'm just sitting at school, everyone just thinking it's fine,
While I'm thinking the world is screaming out,
Shouting all my problems at me.
I want to strut down that corridor,
But I can't, 'cause all I can think about is:
Is my dad okay? Is he alright?
But I have to make everyone at school think I'm fine,
Even though I'm not, not when my dad has cancer.
My mum burst out in tears,
"Your little sister can't find out,
'Cause she's just five, she's just five."
When I go to school, I act like I'm okay,
But everyone asks, "What's wrong with you?"
But I don't wanna say,
'Cause I'm just trapped in a black hole.

Elizabeth Chisholm (12)
The Bolsover School, Bolsover

What Makes Me, Me

As I think about my next steps in life,
I wonder where my feet will lead me,
Through the ups and downs of life,
Around every twist and turn.

Every tear that is drawn to my eye,
Every smile on people's faces as they pass me by,
This makes up my personality,
This is what makes me, me.

Every life brought into our family,
Everyone we have loved,
And who we have lost,
Through no fault of their own.

Loved ones watch from heaven,
As I take new paths in life,
I wonder which way I should go,
What way will my feet lead me?

Every tear that is drawn to my eye,
Every smile on people's faces as they pass me by,
This makes up my personality,
This is what makes me, me.

Lillie-May Crawford (14)
The Bolsover School, Bolsover

This Is Me

I know a girl called Lily,
Just eleven years old,
She's a friend who's always there,
Her kindness is untold.

With sparkling blue eyes,
Incredible grace,
And a beautiful smile,
That lights up her face.

But behind her eyes,
Lie worries of her own,
She feels insecure and nervous,
And doesn't want to leave home.

Afraid of new school beginnings,
And what changes they may bring,
Lily faces them with courage,
As she bravely spreads her wings.

Although she struggles with school,
She's determined to break free,
Of all that holds her back,
She will not turn and flee.

I am Lily,
This is *me!*

Lily Ashley (11)
The Bolsover School, Bolsover

This Is Me

This is me.
I try to find myself in a calm environment,
I don't get out that much.
I come from love and jumping off sofas,
And playing on the swing.
I come from school becoming better every day,
And friends to wake up to, even on holiday.
I am made of my love for my pets,
My dogs and cats and even my snail.
This is me.
I love basketball and sometimes dodgeball.
I love RE, English, PE and maths,
And even history.
I am excited for every day of form,
And most classes I have.
I feel calm around my brothers,
Not my younger one, he is loud!
But my older one, he's nice.
This is me.
I am made from anger, sadness and happiness.
This is me.

Isla Layton (12)
The Bolsover School, Bolsover

I Am Me

I am not like them or you,
You, me, no one's the same,
My name has two 'A' vowels,
Which is different to what it's 'supposed to'.
I come from love and laughter,
Laughter that lies in the memories I've made.
I spend all my time playing sports,
Achieving, performing and conquering along the way.
I love being with my friends,
Friends who know me inside out.
Me and my family are always out,
Motocross, cheerleading and jetskiing,
Are what we're about.
My story is filled with chapters,
Chapters of love, sports, laughter,
Memories and friends.
For I am not like them or you,
Our stories are not the same.

Fraya Pope (14)
The Bolsover School, Bolsover

I Wonder

In a world of colour, I am Isabel, you see,
With hair like sunshine and eyes as blue as the sea.

I love to draw and let my imagination roar.
Creating art that's full of wonder and much, much more.

My sense of humour is a bit silly and bright,
I laugh at jokes that make the day feel light.

Animals forever; furry, finned and scaled are all allowed,
With them, I find joy that makes my heart feel proud.

My stories in books, what a great idea!
Solving puzzles and my stories, I read late into the night.

Stories and tales, I get lost in the thrill,
As Isabel the dreamer, I always will.

Isabel Watkinson (12)
The Bolsover School, Bolsover

Shining Star

I am Matilda,
What people don't know is I have joint problems,
It hurts a lot,
But I get a lot of help from my dad and mum.

But the one person I can rely on is Mabel.
Mabel, my shining star,
You can't give her a label,
Her slobbery wet but warm kisses calm me.

People aren't always kind,
Bullies always make me feel negligible,
If I feel my happiness has descended,
Mabel, my shining star, comes through.

Whatever they say, it doesn't matter,
They may not like who I want to be,
But Mabel, my shining star, comes through,
This is me, Matilda Gibbons!

Matilda Gibbons (11)
The Bolsover School, Bolsover

Judgemental

People are always going to be judged,
From the colour of their hair,
To the way that they speak,
To the way that they look.

To them, it doesn't matter what's inside,
They never look them in the eye.
It doesn't matter what's inside,
Second chances are mostly denied.

But being judgemental just isn't right,
There is no reason to start this fight.
You should give everyone a chance,
To see what they're like.

See beyond the things you can see,
Their talents, their interests,
Their individuality.

Thomas Bowley (12)
The Bolsover School, Bolsover

Who Am I?

William Day, who is he?
He's being assessed for ADHD.
Where you see red, he sees brown,
He sees the world upside down.
He's colour-blind and has autism,
But that doesn't make him much different to you!

He has three cool friends and loves to draw,
A big T-rex, his favourite dinosaur.
Lasagne is the best, pizza too,
He also loves a big bowl of stew.
His favourite subjects are science and art,
He loves to play games in the dark.

This is me, William Day!

William Day (11)
The Bolsover School, Bolsover

Belief

B efore I was bathed in the holy light and love of the Lord,
I was lost in this large endless world
E verything was daunting, everything was thrown at you
L ove is what religion is about and family who love and care
I am a sinner but I believe I have been saved
E ven though the Lord knows I have sinned, He still loves with his omnibenevolence
F inally, I will say it is not just about prayer or belief; so love thy neighbour and family, but also to forgive.

Calum Boyne (16)
The Bolsover School, Bolsover

Is This Who I Am?

I am waiting for the sunrise
I keep my distance from cars
I am waiting for a disguise
Who am I?

The memories keep my family together
My brother is my saviour - my parents do the most
Awakening at midday
Disconnected from the haters in my life
Who am I?

I once was a lazy person
My future was a dream
I'm stuck in the past
Just waiting for the last
When I looked back in time
My life was frozen in time
Who am I?

Shaniya St Clair (11)
The Bolsover School, Bolsover

How To Fit In

Even when your head's in the mud,
There are people who will help,
And make you feel understood.
When you are running away from those who are mean,
Tell someone, wipe your worries clean.
You always have belonged,
And always will.
People are here to right the wrongs,
Teamwork makes the dream work,
So, find your team.
Whether you're big or small,
You can feel misunderstood,
Come on, get your head out of the mud.

Addison Toyne (11)
The Bolsover School, Bolsover

This Is Me

I'm tall, I play football, this is me,
I like dogs but I don't like frogs, that's me!
I'm a drama queen,
That's why I'm joining the drama team.
Yes, that's me!
I like playing with my friends,
But I also like staying in bed and lying in.
That's also me!
I support the England team, especially the goalie,
Well, I am one myself, or I used to be.
I am who I am and that's what I like about me.

Kadee Morley (11)
The Bolsover School, Bolsover

This Is Me

Hi, I'm Chelsee,
And here are lots of things about me:
I have a best friend called Kelsie,
She means the world to me,
Whenever I need her, she is always there for me.
I also have my other friends;
Brooke, Jazmine, Sofia and Grace,
They are all really nice,
I love them lots, so thank you to them!
I have an older brother and a younger sister
(Which is so annoying!).
I also have a dog called Barney who is one.

Chelsee MD (11)
The Bolsover School, Bolsover

The Blacknells

Riley Blacknell is my name,
And my family isn't lame.
I have a funny brother,
And a sound mother.
My dad is the boss,
And trust me, you don't want to make him cross.
We love Man City,
My mum even watches because the boys are pretty!
I play for two football teams,
And being a footballer is part of my dreams.
If I don't make it pro,
I'd like to join the army to make some dough.

Riley Blacknell (11)
The Bolsover School, Bolsover

This Is Me

I am Heidi Gill,
I am funny, kind and helpful,
I like to read and I love sleeping,
I am 11 and I am amazing,
I like making up stories and drawing,
And playing with my Barbie,
I love to go on my Xbox.
And I love to bake cakes and buns,
Oh, and cheesecakes!
I help to feed my pet rabbit.
I play games on my laptop,
And help by tidying up my room.
I also like to listen to music.

Heidi Gill (11)
The Bolsover School, Bolsover

Winston

My best friend, Winston,
I have a Frenchie called Winston.
He dances for attention,
I thought I'd give it a mention.
His face is like a seal,
Roast beef is his favourite meal.
His bad breath,
Is enough to cause sudden death.
His loud snore,
Makes us think someone's at the door.
He hops and skips,
And shakes his little hips.
That's my best friend, Winston.

Archie Shannon (11)
The Bolsover School, Bolsover

This Is Me

My name is Tayla, I'm eleven years old.
I'm a sporty person and I love football,
I just love watching it.
But as well, I like working out and exercising,
It is my favourite thing.
When I was born, I was very poorly,
And almost didn't make it.
I had four holes in my heart.
I am so lucky to still be here today,
And I am so grateful.

Tayla Price (11)
The Bolsover School, Bolsover

This Is Me!

I am me,
To a perfect T,
I am not perfect,
Not a prefect,
But that's okay with me.

At the end of the day,
There is no better way,
Of living,
If you are forgiving.

If you have passion,
Nothing will matter to you,
Not even your fashion.

You can be you,
If I can be me.

Mia-Jade Freeman (11)
The Bolsover School, Bolsover

This Is Me

This is me, this is me,
My favourite colour is light pink.
This is me, this is me,
My favourite animal is a dog,
I like the way they're so cute and cuddly.
This is me, this is me,
My favourite food is spicy curry,
I like the way it tastes.
So that is me and I'm the way I want to be.

Ava Turner (11)
The Bolsover School, Bolsover

This Is Me

I like gaming, it is my hobby
S ometimes I do other things like drawing
A nd I love foods like pasta, pizza, eggs, chicken and burgers
A lso, I enjoy playing out with my friends
C hristmas is my favourite time of the year that I enjoy with my family.

Isaac Unwin (11)
The Bolsover School, Bolsover

This Is Me: I Am...

This is me,
Who I want to be,
Not who you think,
I may be,
I like shopping and basketball,
And I'm always willing to help the team,
And follow my wildest dreams,
I am not who you think I am,
This is me,
And I'll be who I want to be.

Frankie Dunraven (11)
The Bolsover School, Bolsover

I Am...

I am:
Smart,
Amazing,
Talented,
Gorgeous,
Kind,
Caring,
Loved,
Happy,
Moody,
Angry,
Tired,
Short,
Peaceful,
I love to draw,
Respectful,
Unique,
And
I am my own person!

Bianca Onca (11)
The Bolsover School, Bolsover

The Foods I Hate

F ish fingers
O lives
O nions
D ried fruit
S pring rolls.

Leah Haberfield (11)
The Bolsover School, Bolsover

Addiction

I don't want to do it but the thought daunts me.
It hangs above my head like a single storm cloud.
The nagging thoughts of self-sabotage.

Just do it one more time.
One month clear.

I'm proud but I still hate it.
Recovery is a road of twists and turns;
So powerful that sometimes I feel nauseous.

Stephen Baxter (14)
The Gateway School, Tiffield